A WARDEN'S WAY

The Story of Lyle Smith, Maine's "Flying Warden"

A WARDEN'S WAY

The Story of Lyle Smith, Maine's "Flying Warden"

by LYLA E. ST. LOUIS

NORTH COUNTRY PRESS
■ UNITY, MAINE ■

Library of Congress Cataloging-in-Publication Data

St. Louis, Lyla E., 1918–
A warden's way : the life of Lyle Smith of Mount Desert Island /
by Lyla E. St. Louis.
p. cm.
ISBN 0-945980-30-2 : $11.95
1. Smith, Lyle E. 2. Game wardens—Maine—Mount Desert Island—
Biography. 3. Maine Warden Service—Officials and employees—
Biography. I. Title.
SK354.S65S7 1991
363.2'8'092—dc20
[B] 91-8822
CIP

The Publishers express their appreciation to the
Department of Inland Fisheries and Wildlife for its assistance.
Cover design by Ralph Lizotte.
Composition by Camden Type 'n Graphics, Camden, Maine.
Manufactured in the United States of America.
 Address inquiries to North Country Press, P.O. Box 440, Belfast, ME 04915.

DEDICATION

In memory of my father
Game Warden Lyle E. Smith
for his unswerving dedication to duty and
the preservation of wildlife, which knew no limits,
and to my mother, Zettie,
who staunchly supported him.

ACKNOWLEDGEMENT

My sincere appreciation to my sister, Allison, and my friend, Gloria, for their helpful suggestions, advice and editing of this writing.

MAINE WARDEN SERVICE
□ WARDEN'S CREED □

Recognizing the responsibilities entrusted to me as a member of the Warden Service of the Department of Inland Fisheries and Wildlife of the State of Maine, an organization dedicated to the preservation of the fish and game of Maine, I pledge myself to perform my duties honestly and faithfully to the best of my ability and without fear, favor, or prejudice.

I will wage unceasing war against violation of the Fish and Wildlife law in every form and will consider no sacrifice too great in the performance of my duty.

I will obey the laws of the United States of America, and of the State of Maine, and will support and defend their constitutions against all enemies whomsoever, foreign or domestic. I will always be loyal to and uphold the honor of my organization, my state, and my country.

PROLOGUE

Early Man was a hunter. He had to be, for a primary source of food for him on this youthful Planet Earth was the flesh of the animals that he himself hunted and killed.

But this early walker of the woods had an innate sense of conservation and he killed only enough to supply himself and his kind. He did not overkill as his modern descendants are known to do.

In the early days of exploration and settling of the land that was to become America, one of the greatest causes of friction between the Indian and the White Man–the Newcomer–was the latter's thoughtless destruction of wildlife, the land and the forests. The Indian knew that the ruination of these natural resources would cause wildlife to eventually disappear.

The Newcomer, for example, trapped fur-bearing animals, especially the beaver, almost to extinction, and it took years for the beaver to repopulate the species. They were never again, however, to enjoy the numbers they had experienced prior to the arrival of the Newcomer. Moreover, small settlements were mushrooming into large cities because of the fur trade, and the growing demand for furs soon resulted in trapping at even greater levels than before.

Meanwhile the Indians' very existence continued to depend on the land and its fish and meat-producing and fur-bearing animals for food, warmth and shelter. They were wise in the ways of conservation and preservation; they knew full well their people would be endangered unless the sources of their survival were protected.

Man, like any animal, reacts to the forces of nature, but his higher brain development and an ability to record and study his explorations, studies and experiences over time have allowed him to control his environment and to make it responsive, to some extent, to his own needs. But instead of cherishing the environment as the *giver* of life as the Indian did, instead of trying to enhance and safeguard it, the Newcomer and *his* descendants have treated the earth as a sometime-rival. They have used it for their own gain, extracted its precious resources, and when it is no longer of any use, they have abandoned it.

From his self-appointed perch atop life's ladder, Man has looked upon all forms of animal life as inferior. Natural resources are not allowed to play their part in an overall scheme of environmental harmony, but are viewed solely from the perspective of how to make self-serving use of them. His whims have destroyed plants and land-forms, as well as animals. Panthers, buffaloes, and grizzly bears have given way to the westward expansion of agriculture. Hawks and owls are being eliminated by chemicals and sprays, and creatures of marsh and forest are constantly losing their habitats to residential and industrial development and expansion.

Throughout the years, as hunting has become a sport, rather than a necessity of life, Man has become overzealous and greedy in his hunting and fishing pursuits. As a result, federal and state governments have been compelled to initiate and pass laws to protect wildlife.

With the emergence of these laws arose the need for game wardens to enforce them.

Maine, a vastly wooded state covering more than 33,000 square miles, once abounded in wild game. Its hundreds of lakes, rivers, and streams bulged with fish, and its dense forests were rich with both large and small animals. This was prime territory in which to profit by the taking of both fish and game. Hunters found an eager market for moose, deer, and caribou in the large cities to the south and west of Maine.

Maine began to consider protective fish and game laws in the 1870's, but at that time the laws pertained only to the taking of fish, and the so-called fish wardens had no authority regarding the protection of game. Even though a law was passed at that time limiting the taking of deer to three per year, there were not enough wardens for proper enforcement. Nor did the Department of Inland Fisheries and Game have funds available to delegate the power of game enforcement to the fish wardens.

In 1880, Maine's governor, Alonzo Garcelon, was authorized to appoint wardens whose duty it was to enforce both fish and game laws. As time went on, there was still very little money in the Department, and wardens in the Maine Warden Service held other jobs and worked as wardens only when time permitted. The rewards of the job were small and the wardens were reimbursed very poorly from fines collected from the few lawbreakers that they did manage to apprehend. And it was a risky business at best, for a number of wardens were attacked and beaten by poachers. Consequently, being a game warden was not a popular job in those early years.

In the early 1900's a hunting and fishing license fee was levied upon non-residents, and this extra revenue helped to improve the Warden Service. Later on, residents also were required to buy hunting and fishing licenses.

By the 1930's, the Maine Warden Service had emerged as a well-established department under the guidance and leadership of George J. Stobie, who held the position of commissioner of the Department of Inland Fisheries and Game for 21 years, from 1929 to

1950. In those years, Stobie saw the annual budget rise from $250,000 to $1,000,000. He was aware of the ever-increasing pressures on Maine's fish and wildlife. Under his direction, the development of fishery research and law enforcement programs was widely expanded. He established the Wildlife Research Division within the Department and later on, the Fishery Research and Management Division.

Stobie had the foresight and the ability to initiate action in setting up foundations for scientific management of fish and game, as well as modern conservation law enforcement throughout the state.

Throughout his administration, he constantly built upon that base and further enhanced the structure of the then Department of Inland Fisheries and Game.

Everything that the Department of Inland Fisheries and Wildlife is today rests solely upon the firm foundation that Stobie laid for it. Throughout the Pine Tree State, sportsmen, conservationists and lovers of its natural magnificence will be forever indebted to him.

Early in his career as commissioner, Stobie started upgrading the Maine Warden Service and therein begins the story of my father, Warden Lyle Ernest Smith, who served in the Maine Warden Service on Mount Desert Island from 1928 to 1953.

1

How well I remember that warm summer day in 1928 when two affluent-looking men drove into our yard and asked to see my father! I was only ten then and bubbling over with childish curiousity. My father told us children to run along and play and to be very quiet. We sat under the big maple tree on the front lawn, whispering and speculating about why those two strangers had come. We were a bit awestruck by their impressive appearance and bearing.

Finally, my father, mother, and the two prosperous-looking gentlemen emerged from the house. The men shook hands with my parents, and congratulated my father. As soon as they had departed we were happily informed that Daddy had been appointed to the Maine Warden Service. I also learned some years later that the two men who came to the house that day were Commissioner George J. Stobie and Joseph Stickney, Chief Warden. During the years of my father's warden service, I was to see both many times.

The elation my family felt that day was indescribable! My dad a game warden! He loved the forest and its creatures and forever instilled in us children the need to respect nature. We loved to listen to him talk about conservation and preservation of our natural resources as we sat around our big round oak dining table after dinner.

Most of my conscious life Daddy had been a farmer on Mount Desert Island, where he had lived since he was sixteen. Before that his family had lived in the town of Franklin where his ancestors were the first settlers. When he was sixteen the family moved to Northeast Harbor on Mount Desert Island, since my Grandfather Smith had obtained work there as a carpenter, which was his trade. When World War I was declared, my father, Lyle, then eighteen, immediately enlisted in the navy. During this time, he met my mother, Luzetta Swazey, a Bar Harbor girl, and they were married in September, 1917. In August, 1918, I made my appearance on this planet. After the armistice was signed in November, 1918, Lyle was discharged from the navy. He then went to work for a very prominent summer family in Northeast Harbor as a chauffeur. He worked there for a couple of years until the lady of the family died, at which time he decided to buy a small farm and go into business for himself. He kept a small dairy herd and delivered dairy products, vegetables and poultry to summer residents and hotels in Northeast Harbor.

The farm was located between Bar Harbor and Ellsworth, in an area then called West Eden, and now known as Town Hill. West Eden was a small village with two general stores, a two-room schoolhouse, a grange hall and a church: a real country town of less than 200 "salt of the earth" people who formed a closely-knit community.

Most of the local men were employed on the big summer estates in Bar Harbor and Northeast Harbor during the summer as these towns were then in their heyday as wealthy summer resorts.

In the long, cold winters some of the men worked in the woods, as wood was the main source of fuel in those days.

In 1919, a part of Mount Desert Island was declared a national park, called Lafayette National Park. It was later renamed Acadia National Park and at that time was the only national park east of the Mississippi. After this occurred, there was a great deal of employment due to bequests by John D. Rockefeller, Sr., whose generosity then made possible the beautiful carriage roads around the island and the famous road up Cadillac Mountain, the highest of the granite mountains along the eastern coast. The construction of these roads provided employment for island residents for many years. Lyle worked on the Cadillac Mountain Road for a period of time during the fall and winter months when work on the farm was less demanding. At this time, too, in the 1920's, he worked as a "nonpaid" warden or deputy for the state, a volunteer service given by men who were dedicated to preserving the state's wildlife. No doubt this was a factor in his being appointed to the Maine Warden Service. In this capacity he had done volunteer work with the only two rangers employed by the National Park Service on the island at that time. I'm sure their recommendations to the commissioner were powerful factors as well.

His time spent in carrying out his duties as a "nonpaid" warden stood him in good stead for the twenty-five years he served in the Warden Service. The woods, fields, lakes and streams of the island were as familiar to him as the back of his hand. His territory then included not only Mount Desert Island, but parts of "Down East" on the mainland as far as Schoodic Point. This was a vast area for one man to cover to carry out his duties, which were many and varied.

Deer-hunting season provided quite a challenge to stamina and time as deer hunting was legal on the mainland, but not on Mount Desert. It was a designated deer sanctuary throughout the whole island, though hunting for small game animals was legal at specified times during the year. However, no hunting of any kind was permissable in the national park area. This was a problem too, as deer poachers did not always know the park boundaries and if they were caught within the confines of the park, poaching deer, it was a federal offense, resulting in a much harsher penalty. Lyle once had to arrest

A formal portrait from the 1940's of Warden Division F, District 31, Ellsworth, Me. Front row (l-r): Fred Smith, Raymond Harrington, Raymond Morse (Supervisor), Wilbur Ricker, Hollis Patterson, Lyle Smith. Back row (l-r): George Bradbury, Clinton Barrett, Wallace Barron.

the son of a National Park Service official for hunting in the national park. That caused quite a stir around town and around MDI!

It was a common saying hereabouts that Lyle Smith would arrest his own mother if he caught her breaking a fish or game law. That I would not doubt for a minute, for he did arrest his brother-in-law one November night. A neighbor who lived about a mile away phoned to say that shots had just been fired in her field. Lyle dashed to the area and there, crouched in a ditch beside the road, preparing to load a deer, was a man trying desperately to keep out of sight. Lyle jumped from the car, flashing a light in his direction. There he was lying on top of a big buck that he had unsuccessfully tried to drag behind a clump of bushes a few feet away, as Lyle's car approached.

"What in hell are you doing here?" Lyle exclaimed as he recognized Brother-in-Law. "Haven't you enough sense to know where night hunting will get you?"

Sheepishly, Brother-in-Law admitted, "Well, I've been tramping the woods in Trenton all day and didn't see a thing, so when this buck crossed the road in front of me, the temptation was too great. I couldn't help myself as I didn't want to go home empty-handed." He lived near Portland and had come down to hunt in Trenton on the mainland that day.

As it turned out, he had a companion with him who had taken to the woods when he saw Lyle.

Lyle took Brother-in-Law and deer back to the house and called in the state police to search for his friend. Within a few minutes the friend appeared at the door and shamefacedly said, "I figured I'd better turn myself in as Lyle always gets his man, and I'm in enough hot water already."

Both of them had their rifles confiscated and were fined $200 or thirty days in jail. The friend who had skedaddled couldn't come up with the $200 fine so he served the thirty days. As Brother-in-Law later stated, "We could have bought a helluva lot of beef for what that hunting trip cost us."

Even though Lyle was a stickler for enforcing the fish and game laws, his veins could run with the milk of human kindness when the occasion arose. He was known to look the other way when he saw a man dragging out an illegally shot deer, knowing the man hadn't worked for months and had a hungry family at home. Times were tough during the '30's and work was scarce. When deer were so plentiful, it was hard to see one's family going hungry for want of meat and the temptation was great and worth the risk.

One time Lyle received a complaint about a neighbor cooking deer meat for supper, so he made an unexpected call just at suppertime. The poor wife was standing over a hot stove frying up a big pan of venison and shaking like a leaf when Lyle came to the door. A passel of undernourished children sat around the table waiting for supper. Lyle had smelled the venison cooking before he entered the house. He passed the time of day for a few minutes, then as he turned to leave, he said, "It doesn't smell like deer meat to me." Then he opened the door and walked out.

Another time he dropped in on a neighbor who was also in dire straits for lack of work and who also had small children. They saw him drive in just as the fry pan full of venison was about done. The old woodstove was blazing away and the smell of the venison wafted through the air. As Lyle approached, the wife lifted the stove cover and dumped the whole fry pan full of meat right into the fire. When Lyle opened the door the odor of burned meat met his nostrils. "That's too bad to waste that good meat, Maggie," he said. Not another word was said by him about it then or ever. The neighbors later told about it.

One time, much to his chagrin, he was outfoxed by some poachers, which upset him no end to think he had been so easily duped. A person in a nearby town made a complaint to Lyle that certain of his neighbors were poaching deer, eating venison with great relish and boasting to him about it. Being a law-abiding citizen he came to Lyle, who then procured a search warrant, and along with a park ranger, proceeded to search the premises. They found nothing—not even a clue, after a very intensive search. A short time later, gossip got back to Lyle that he and the ranger had walked over the evidence several times. It had been buried in a snow bank beside the road where the snowplow had thrown back the snow. Who would have thought to look there? Another time he wouldn't be so gullible. Years later he laughed about it as being a good joke on him.

Lyle poses in his first uniform, 1928.

2

I will never forget the day my father arrived home in his new uniform. He strutted around as proud as a peacock so all the family could admire him. His long, lean, six-foot frame looked really impressive with the Sam Browne belt strapped around his waist and over his left shoulder, and a leather holster containing a .38 caliber pistol hanging from the belt. His officer's hat sat low over his deep blue eyes and his long legs were encased in shiny black puttees over officer's breeches. The uniform was a light oxford gray wool and very well-fitted. I was awe-struck by the authority he displayed and I thought he was the handsomest man alive.

Lyle's appointment to the Maine Warden Service occurred during the Great Depression and we thought we were two-thirds wealthy to have a steady income. His starting pay was $125 per month with no allowance for travel expenses, and he had to use his own car. State–owned vehicles were not assigned to wardens in those early years. Later, he received a small expense account to help with mileage. With all the miles he traveled just to patrol his territory, it's a good thing gas was cheap. Sometimes you could buy ten gallons for a dollar but it was normally five gallons for a dollar. During price wars I've seen it up to twelve gallons for a dollar. That is hard to believe when we think of gas prices today.

Gradually, Lyle's life changed from being a farmer to being a well-known and highly respected law enforcement officer. I think it is a fair statement to say that he became a fanatic about his work: it was a way of life to which he became more dedicated as time passed. He gave no thought to long hours or overtime by today's standards. No matter how many hours the job required, he did it with no thought of reimbursement. This dedication to duty surpassed all else, except, I should say, his family. He was death on poachers and night hunters and in the '30's they were plentiful. Work was scarce and people needed food. Many had no intention of obeying the game laws. They had never bothered to obey them before a game warden appeared on the scene and didn't plan to change their ways at that point. They killed deer whenever the spirit moved them and gave no thought to wildlife preservation. For one thing, many summer people were prime customers for venison and it brought a high price to those daring souls who supplied them. It wasn't unusual to find a deer in the woods with only the hind quarters taken, the remainder of the carcass left to rot. When Lyle ran across such a sight he saw red. If he had ever caught up with the culprit who had killed the animal, I wouldn't want to vouch for his safety.

One thing he could not tolerate was night hunting or jacking deer with a light. He said he had much more respect for a hunter who took his chances hunting in the daytime than for one who used a light to shoot a deer. The animal at least had a sporting chance in daylight, but not when it was blinded by a light. He always said a true sportsman gave his quarry a sporting chance. Many is the time I've heard him say, "Never shoot at a bird unless it is on the wing, or a deer unless it's moving."

As I previously stated, his devotion to duty was paramount in his life. It wasn't out of the ordinary for him to work around the clock, especially in the fall when poaching was rampant on Mount Desert Island. On occasion I've known him to go seventy-two hours without going to bed. He'd catch a catnap sitting upright in a chair, and then be off to a spot where he expected night hunters to appear. Many is the time I've dropped him off at a certain spot under cover of darkness, with his sleeping bag and a Thermos of coffee, where he would spend the night waiting for a culprit. Before daylight, I would pick him up and then hurry home to catch the school bus into Bar Harbor for high school.

When Lyle was away, after his appointment to the Warden Service, the lot of milking our old cow fell to me. I was the oldest of the five children, so I was assigned the most responsible duties. We had kept one cow to supply the family's needs after he gave up farming. I didn't like the job as I was afraid I'd smell like the barn when I went to school. However, I arose early, did the barn work, then scrubbed myself rosy red to make sure I was scent-free. There were some other kids who worked in barns before they went to school, and when they got on the school bus each morning, we all held our noses. Later on, my mother learned to milk and took over the job, much to my great relief.

The old cow was over twenty when she fell down in the barn and broke two legs. Lyle knew she was getting mighty old, but he'd had her around so long he couldn't bring himself to part with her. She was still a good milker despite her long life. Luckily for him, the day she broke her legs he was away on duty, so my mother got a kind neighbor to shoot the cow and haul her off before Lyle arrived home. He was relieved that the sad deed hadn't been left to him. He hated to kill anything and our chickens practically died from old age unless my mother could find a neighbor to kill them for her. On occasion, she did it herself, though it wasn't exactly to her liking. She had five hungry mouths to feed and those chickens were eating us out of house and home. Lyle would keep a pig to be slaughtered only if he boarded up one side of the pen and made a sluice for the food to be poured into. If he had to see the pig he could never butcher it for our consumption. After we children were grown and had left home, he said to my mother, "I'm some glad I don't have to raise a pig any more and have him squealing his head off when he sees me coming with his food, and then have to kill him later."

Lyle would starve before he'd eat venison. Once a neighbor brought us some, unbeknown to him. My sister from New York was visiting at the time and decided to cook it for dinner. He sat there enjoying his "steak" immensely until my sister told him what he was eating. He flew into a rage such as I have never seen. He threw the dishes across the table and yelled at my sister for playing such a dirty trick on him. It really frightened us and I'm sure my sister would think twice before she pulled such a trick again. She knew how he felt about venison and thought it was a good joke on him. I'm surprised he didn't recognize what he was eating before she told him, but it probably didn't enter his mind that it could be venison.

During World War II keeping up with poachers on Mount Desert Island was a problem. Meat was scarce and deer were overrunning the place. The deer herds had increased so much that they ran over everything like wild cattle. They raised havoc with gardens and every night two or three were struck and killed by cars. At that time the state paid for car damages caused by deer, which ran into many thousands of dollars. Sometimes a driver would elect to take the deer in payment, if the damage was slight. Other times the deer was dressed out and given to public institutions. That was a most unpleasant job if the animal had been badly battered in the accident. Lyle hated it with a passion. Dressing out a deer isn't a pleasant job to begin with, but dressing out one whose insides have been smashed to pieces results in a complete revulsion against venison. I wouldn't be surprised if my father would not eat venison for that reason alone, but the major reason was that we had raised so many orphaned and injured deer, to which he became deeply attached. In fact, all of us played nursemaid to many and varied animals from eagles to beaver, as well as deer.

One day Lyle came home with two yearling beaver that had been trapped from an area that beaver had flooded. He thought they were too young to fend for themselves completely, so he released them in the frog pond near our house where he could keep a watchful eye on them. Young beaver stay with their parents until they are two before choosing a mate and starting their own families. They have much to learn from the adult beaver before they are self-sustaining. All that summer he hauled in poplar limbs for them to eat and they played and frolicked the summer long. Whenever they saw Lyle approaching, they swam to him for all they were worth, their little black eyes and snouts just visible above the water. Their expressions always amused him no end. They knew where their food came from. As cold weather approached, Lyle was concerned that they might not be able to survive the winter unless they built a lodge, which he feared they were too young to know how to do. Besides, they needed access to poplar trees. He decided to trap them out and transfer them to another area with other beaver, where they would have an adequate supply of "popple" to see them through the cold weather, and also where they would learn to build a lodge.

Another time he came home toting a young eagle that had an injured wing. We had a box stall in the barn where the bird was kept until its injured wing healed. It consumed pounds of hamburger. Finally, one day, after several weeks of captivity, Lyle felt the eagle was well enough to fly. It seemed to be using the wing normally just flying around the stall. When Lyle opened the barn door to freedom, the eagle came zooming out and took off in a burst of speed. For a minute after he gained altitude, he circled over the barn a couple of times, crying his raucous scream as if to say thank you. Then soaring high, he gradually vanished to a tiny dot as he blended into the bright blue sky.

One early summer morning Lyle came home with a young seal. He had been watching the little fellow for a couple of days and it had remained in the same place on the shore. The mother seemed to have deserted it. The poor little thing was crying piteously so Lyle could stand it no longer. He brought him home. We named him "Solomon Seal" and what an adorable pet he was! Seals are so intelligent! Lyle put him in a big wooden metal-lined sink that had been used in the milkroom in farming days, hauling salt water, seaweed and what have you, to keep him wet. Every day we kids took him to the ocean to swim. We carried him a mile each way and Solomon was no lightweight even at that young age. He was such fun to play with in the water. He would dive under us, jump over us, and if we floated on our backs he was likely to flop right on top of us, looking us right in the eye with those big, limpid brown eyes, which always reminded me of velvety brown pansies. We had Solomon for about six weeks, but one morning when we went to his pen we found him dead. He had seemed fine the night before, but Lyle said he probably had had something wrong with him anyway, and that was the reason the mother deserted him. For a few weeks we had enjoyed a wonderful pet.

Today orphaned seals are taken to the New England Aquarium in Boston, where they are given proper care and diet and seem to do very well. It is difficult to raise a seal in captivity without knowing scientifically what its diet should consist of. We sure weren't aware of that at the time and that could have been another reason he didn't survive.

Another time Lyle came across a young doe spread-eagled on the ice. She was nearly dead from exposure but he gathered her up in a blanket, brought her home, and put her in the empty horse stall in the barn. After several days of warmth and constant care, she started to eat. Each day she became stronger and more tame. She was warm and comfortable there and soon fully regained her strength. She dined on apples, carrots, lettuce, cabbage and many tasty tidbits—a far cry from her food in the wild, which she would have had to forage to find, and in winter is hard to come by. As early spring approached, Lyle felt she was strong enough to be freed It was a warm March day, though some snow still remained on the ground. Lyle opened the barn doors, waiting for her to come out. Soon she came trotting to the door where she hesitated for a minute, looking out at the snowy scene before her. Suddenly she turned and trotted right back to the stall. Lyle said she had had such a good winter, she wasn't about to go out and face snow again, so she kept her comfortable quarters for another month or so until the warmth of spring arrived and the snow had disappeared. Then one late April day, Lyle opened the door once more. Again she came to the door, surveyed the scene before her, and this time bounded out the door and across the back field to the woods, all the time waving adieu with her white flag. Another deer saved from a ghastly death!

We saved many deer from cruel deaths. Our most famous one was called Bambi, whom I'll tell you more about later on in this book.

There was a lady who owned a summer cottage on the western shore of Long Pond where she lived from early June to late October. During those months she kept bird feeders full of seeds for the wild birds. Hundreds of them visited the feeders and to watch and identify them was a great source of pleasure to her. As cold weather approached and she prepared to leave for her winter home near Boston, she became concerned about the birds' welfare. She had fed them all during the good months when food was easy to find, and now with cold weather coming on and natural food becoming scarce, she was worried. She turned to Lyle to seek his advice. He quickly offered to go to her cottage every other day to fill the feeders if she could leave a supply of food where he would have access to it. This was happily arranged and Lyle took on the responsibility of feeding her fine-feathered friends. This was no easy task once the deep snows came. The cottage was a good mile and a half off the main road and her road was not plowed in winter. Then Lyle donned his snowshoes and made the trip three times a week. He, too, got great pleasure from this, as the birds became so tame. Before he was anywhere near the cottage, they would come swarming, swooping and chirping to meet him. The chickadees were the charmers. He wore a wide-brimmed Stetson hat, part of a new uniform issue, which was identical to the type worn by the Canadian Mounties. As the chickadees flocked to greet him, they landed around the rim of his hat and up and down his shoulders, chirping and singing away as they enjoyed a snowshoe trek to the cottage. Some would gently peck him on the cheek like a caress as he trekked along. He got such enjoyment and delight from their exuberant and joyful greetings that he kept up this feeding routine for quite a few years until the poor lady passed away, and a new owner took over.

3

Two-way radios were not yet available to wardens during Lyle's years in the Service; if they had been, more night hunters could have been apprehended, and the wardens' work would have been greatly simplified. Scores of hunters escaped as there was no way of intercepting them quickly.

Lyle had numerous and varied tales about his apprehension of night hunters. Some of them were quite embarrassing, to say the least. Others were violent and alarming. Some were comical.

He frequently worked with the park rangers in their quests for poachers and lawbreakers. One night he was working with Ranger Orient Thompson. They had seen daylight signs of poachers in an old deserted field where there once had been a farm and a large orchard—a haven for poachers as apples were plentiful and a perfect spot for deer to frequent. This particular early autumn night, the two men had driven to the orchard, concealed their car some distance away, and settled down in their sleeping bags to await the unwary hunters. About 10:00 P.M. they heard another car approaching. It drove up through the orchard and stopped, leaving the headlights on, which could be a sign of night hunters jacking deer. They waited a few minutes to give the hunters time to load their guns, which would be positive evidence. Then they rushed the car, each going to an opposite side. They yanked the doors open and to their great amazement found a prominent town businessman making violent love to an exceedingly corpulent lady, a cook from one of the summer cottages. Talk about being surprised! The man was in a state of shock, as he was well acquainted with both officers. He begged and pleaded with them not to tell about his transgression. Lyle never mentioned the man's name, but he did tell my mother about the incident. When he got home that night, he sat on the edge of the bed removing his shoes and socks, still shaking with laughter remembering the man's expression. He laughed so hard, the bed shook, and that woke my mother. "Lyle, whatever are you laughing about?" she inquired. Between gasps of laughter, he related the story to her and, no doubt, told her who it was, but the man's secret was safe with them. I'm sure the man shook in his shoes for days.

A similar situation occurred another autumn night when Lyle and Ory were hidden in the woods bordering an open field and orchard in a remote area where deer were often spotted. They detected a car parked near some apple trees and crept quietly across the open space. They used the same tactics in jumping the car, each to an opposite side. When Lyle jerked open the door on the passenger's side, he expected to find someone with a loaded gun ready for action. Instead, out fell a stark-naked couple clasped in a tight embrace. They flopped around on the ground bewilderedly for a few seconds trying to comprehend what had happened. The girl emitted blood-curdling screams, while the fellow let loose with a string of oaths that would make a pirate look as if he were studying his Sunday school lesson.

"Excuse us!" exclaimed Lyle. "We thought you were night hunters." The couple scrambled back into the car and Lyle and Ory cleared out of there in a hurry. An embarrassing situation, but all in a day's work.

Another time Lyle and Ory had an area staked out for poachers and went to the spot just at dusk. On his way to the area, Lyle had stopped to check a beaver trap which he had set that morning to trap out beaver that were damming up a culvert, causing the highway to flood over. These were "live" traps which did not harm the animal, but allowed the warden to remove it to another place where it could do no damage. In the trap he found a yearling beaver, so he loaded him, trap and all, into the back seat of the old Model A Ford. He planned to liberate him in the morning in a suitable place. He met Ory and they retired to an inconspicuous place with their sleeping bags after he'd driven the car into a small thicket some distance away. In the wee hours of the morning, the tooting of a horn brought them to their feet. It kept up a certain rhythm as they dashed in the direction of the sound. Can you believe it was from Lyle's car? As they approached they made out a small black head just above the steering wheel and heard a rhythmic *Er-rah! Er-rah!* There standing upright on the front seat, his forefeet placed firmly on the horn button, was Baby Beaver. Somehow he had managed to spring open the trap and was having a ball tooting the horn. Lyle said he sure looked comical standing there pushing away, with his beady black eyes peering up at them and a gleeful expression on his face, like a child discovering a new toy.

Another beaver episode turned into a rather scary situation.

Lyle had trapped a big old beaver from a flooded area and planned to transport him to a flowage on Great Cranberry Island, which lies just off the coast of Mount Desert. This beaver must have weighed close to eighty pounds and he was mean. His cutting teeth must have been five inches long which meant he could fell a big tree in no time.

Lyle had made arrangements with Chester Brown, a coastal warden pilot, to fly the animal to Great Cranberry Island. He had transferred the beaver from his wire trap to a larger wooden cage with round slats about an inch and a half in diameter, running from top to bottom. This cage gave the beaver more room to move. I helped Lyle load the cage into the trunk of the car and we started off for the plane, which was waiting on the ramp at Long Pond, four miles away. I told him he should have kept the beaver in the wire trap as he would snap the slats off in one bite each. Lyle scoffed at the idea and said he wouldn't chew them off in such a short time. He was a great one to trust to luck and take chances, but I knew just looking at those teeth, they could work mighty fast. So we started out, the beaver growling and snarling in the trunk of the car. Before we got to Somesville, two miles away, there was such a commotion in the trunk, we knew he had chewed his way out. When we arrived at the plane, Brownie was waiting. Luckily, Lyle had brought the wire trap along as he planned to reset it later, in the same area.

Now here was a big problem: how were they going to get Mr. Beaver from the trunk into the trap? Finally they decided to throw a blanket over him and work him into the trap that way. It took some doing but eventually it was accomplished. It's a good thing beaver are awkward and clumsy animals on land—that one was frightened as well as vicious.

After a brief struggle, Lyle and Brownie got Mr. Beaver aboard the plane. They had been airborne only a few minutes when the trap flew open and out crawled Mr. Beaver, hissing and snarling and rolling about. That's a pretty scary situation: flying 2,000 to 2,500 feet over the open ocean with a mad beaver on the rampage, and mad he was. Again the blanket came to the rescue. Lyle threw it over the beaver and he groped blindly about until Brownie set the plane down at Great Cranberry Island. Once more they maneuvered him into the trap and liberated him in his new home without further ado.

I have always had great sympathy for beaver who are displaced from their home flowages. They form such close-knit families and mate for life unless a mate dies. My father hated trapping beaver but it had to be done when they were damaging property, and it was better to remove them than to destroy the animals. You could blow up their dams one day and the next morning, as if by magic, they would be rebuilt. Even more, he hated to see trappers trapping them for their fur. Trapping is a cruel death because the beaver is pulled under water and drowned as he cannot surface for air. Since they can hold their breath for quite a long time under water, it takes a long time for them to drown. They are determined and persistent animals, and much more intelligent than we humans give them credit for.

Not all of the incidents in which Lyle was involved during his warden's career had to do with enforcing fish and game laws. One he would never forget!

One late summer night when World War II was at its height, he and Ranger Thompson staked out a spot on Ocean Drive where there had been evidence of poachers. Ocean Drive, which lies within the boundaries of Acadia National Park, is a very scenic road which winds along the edge of Frenchman Bay where high cliffs jut out of deep water. There are many narrow inlets that cut into granite bluffs where a boat could anchor and be well-concealed at high tide. This particular night, the two men were snuggled down in their sleeping bags waiting patiently for unsuspecting poachers. In the night stillness, they became aware of the steady throbbing of an engine, which seemed to be coming from a small inlet cut deep into the shoreline, just a short distance from where they lay. Warily, they crept to the edge of the bluff. To their amazement, lying at anchor below was a submarine. It had surfaced in this secluded inlet to recharge its batteries during high tide. Looking down against the background of the sea, they could make out the silhouettes of uniformed men moving about and conversing in muffled tones which Lyle immediately recognized as German. With utmost caution, they crept back to the car which was concealed some distance away. They made a mad dash into Bar Harbor, about five miles away, to report the incident. Needless to say, by the time any action could be taken, the sub had disappeared. The inlet lay deserted and peaceful once again with a slight oil slick sloshing about. I've often wondered what might have happened if Lyle had had the use of a two-way radio then. There was constantly talk during the war of German warships and subs patrolling our coast. After that occurrence, no one had to convince Lyle of the fact. He knew what he'd seen with his own eyes, and each time he told the story, his excitement grew.

When the great fire of October, 1947, nearly devastated Bar Harbor, as well as many acres of Acadia National Park, Lyle was needed to help direct the fire line because of his great knowledge of the island territory. The fire burned for nearly a week before it blazed into the inferno that destroyed seventy summer estates and one hundred seventy year-round homes.

After the fire was under control, I remember Lyle saying it was so terrible to see people's homes burning as their owners stood helpless in a fifty-mile-an-hour gale, but seeing poor, bewildered animals—deer, rabbits, foxes and others trying to flee the holocaust with their fur on fire was a sight he would never forget.

Another incident which happened during the Great Fire of 1947 shows Lyle's firmness of purpose and his power of persuasion.

About a mile from the small village of Town Hill where we lived, the fire was a raging demon and heading straight for our tiny hamlet. Lyle had rounded up about thirty men from the town. They were equipped with shovels, axes and other fire-fighting apparatus and were heading into the territory where the fire was the worst. They were fighting to save their homes and possessions and time was running out.

As Lyle and his contingent approached the fire line, they were halted by a patrol of soldiers from Dow Field in Bangor who wouldn't let them through. Now that was like dangling a red flag before an angry bull! Lyle's blue eyes turned to points of steel, and his countenance took on such a menacing look that the officer in charge was quite taken aback. Who was this man who dared defy the United States Army? Lyle's right hand rested on the butt of his .38 officer's model revolver as he rasped, "We're goin' through and if any of you s.o.b.'s try to stop me, you'll have this to deal with!" He patted his revolver to show he meant business. The soldiers let them pass with no further argument. They got the fire under control at last, helped by a swift change in wind direction.

4

It is probably safe to say that every man in the warden service has had a close brush with death, because firearms nearly always figure in problem situations. The greatest percentage of game law infractions involves hunters; thus, the risk is greater.

Needless to say, Lyle had his share of narrow escapes. Sometimes I think he had more lives than a cat as he managed to get away unscathed countless times.

The nearest he came to meeting his Maker was a night hunting incident in which three hunters were involved.

He had driven his car about 200 feet off the main road into a thickly overgrown woods road where it would not be easily spotted. This was near a deer-crossing over the main highway which was seldom traveled late at night. Shortly, he heard a car approaching from some distance away. About a hundred feet above the entrance to the woods road it stopped and a shot rang out. Lyle crept from his car along the road where he could see two men pulling a deer from the middle of the highway. Their car's motor was still running, prepared for a fast getaway. The only way he could accost them was by approaching directly into the glare of their headlights. He yelled, "Stop! You're under arrest!" So surprised were they that one man bolted for the woods and the other jumped on the running board on the driver's side, yelling, "Let's get the hell out of here!"

At the same time, Lyle jumped on the opposite side of the car, again commanding them to stop. A third man at the wheel hit the gas as the one on the opposite running board reached across, brandishing a five-cell flashlight, hitting Lyle squarely in the face. They traveled about a hundred feet, both men still hanging on, when the driver spied a big spruce tree with limbs hanging over the road. He took dead aim for that tree. The impact knocked Lyle off the running board, and then the car zoomed off into the night, leaving the deer and the hastily-dropped gun still lying in the road. This skirmish left Lyle unconscious for about three hours, and he finally regained consciousness about 1:00 A.M. Being in great shock and pain and covered with blood, he lay there for some time unable to move. In the collision with the tree, he had hit a branch more than two inches in diameter with such force that it broke off right flush to the trunk. He realized he was badly hurt as he had great difficulty getting to his feet, but he managed to crawl and drag himself to where the deer and gun lay. He succeeded by sheer grit in getting them into the ditch. He had to have that evidence! On hands and knees he crawled to the car, which had to be backed out of the narrow woods road, there being no way to turn around. Then he had to drive over eight miles home. How he managed this was beyond me as he had difficulty sitting upright. Later, we found that he had six broken ribs. His back muscles were torn and his face was a bloody, bruised mess. His front teeth were broken and his upper lip had been cut by the flashlight blow, so that it was hanging loose over his lower lip.

I was awakened about 2:30 A.M. by a horn blowing repeatedly in the yard, but half-dulled with sleep, I didn't become alarmed. Eventually, I heard moaning and groaning downstairs in the kitchen. Quickly I ran down, and there was Lyle on his hands and knees, his head on a chair and my mother trying to clean up the blood. The horn had awakened her as well, and she had helped him out of the car. I let out a blood-curdling scream. I thought surely he must be close to death. He was still unable to stand upright and groaned with the slightest movement. He kept repeating between moans, "I've got to get back there! I need that deer and gun for evidence!" My mother insisted that he go to the hospital, but there was no stopping him. He was determined to go back for the evidence. She knew it was futile to argue so she then called a neighbor to help. Lyle crawled back to the car and flopped on the back seat where he was in agony the whole time. The neighbor drove to the scene of the crime where they retrieved the deer and the gun. Only then would Lyle allow my mother to call his supervisor, Raymond Morse, who lived twelve miles away in Ellsworth. Ray was there in just minutes and drove him into Bar Harbor to the hospital where he was bandaged up and kept overnight. In the meantime, wardens and state police were descending upon the scene like flies. Lyle said he could vividly remember the car. It was an old rusty-red Chevrolet coupe he would recognize at once. He said also that one of the men helping to drag the deer out of the road was wearing a black-and-white baseball cap and what stuck in his mind was that his hair was sticking out of the eyelets in the cap. Despite the intense investigating, all the evidence that was found besides the deer and gun was the baseball cap which the fellow lost when he took to the woods.

About six weeks later, a neighbor who was working on a government project near Bass Harbor heard a worker bragging quietly to another worker about how he'd gotten the best of the game warden in a night hunting confrontation a few weeks before.

All this time Lyle had been laid up recovering from his injuries. The neighbor reported what he had heard, gave the fellow's name and said he drove a red Chevrolet such as Lyle remembered. That was all the evidence they needed! When the fellow knew his number was up, he revealed the names of his accomplices. They were all found guilty and duly sentenced in the next term of Superior Court to thirty days in jail and a $200 fine, which in those Depression days was a small fortune. The fellow who lost his cap turned state's evidence in court and received a lighter sentence. Later, he said he had hung around in the woods that night until he saw Lyle regain consciousness, then he took off. He thought they'd killed him and if that had been the case he was getting the hell out of the state. He sure didn't intend to be caught as an accessory in the murder of Lyle Smith.

After that incident, the commissioner set forth an ultimatum that wardens were to work in pairs when looking for night hunters. This was difficult in Lyle's situation since he was the only warden on Mount Desert Island. However, the Acadia National Park rangers were always willing to work with him. It was a reciprocal situation.

Another close call came a few years later. Lyle was working with Ranger Vernon Lunt checking on dogs chasing deer. They had spent the night at the warden's camp at the foot of Western Mountain so they could be up at dawn to look for the offenders, about which there had been many complaints. They had climbed a short distance up the mountain trail when Vern gave Lyle a violent push, sending him sprawling several feet down the mountainside. Lyle looked up in disbelief, wondering what had happened. Then he saw that if he had taken one more step, he would have been blown to glory. Someone had set up a snare gun made from a sawed-off shotgun across a deer trail, and in the glare of the early morning sun, Lyle had failed to see it. Vern was just far enough behind and looking from a different angle so that his eye caught sight of the wire which was attached to the trigger, the gun being well-hidden in the underbrush. If Lyle's foot had tripped that wire, it would have been all over. The culprit was eventually apprehended by keeping the spot under surveillance for a few days. It was a fellow who had originally lived in the northern part of the state, near the Canadian border, where this seemed to be a common practice even though illegal. His big mistake here was to set his snare up in national park territory which made it a federal offense as well as a state infraction. He paid a heavy fine and served a jail sentence. However, he never held a grudge against Lyle and apologized profusely to him many times. I clearly recall the man weeping wildly at my father's funeral and sobbing, "Lyle Smit was ze bes' fren' I ever had!"

Another incident happened when I was about eleven years old, shortly after my father had entered the warden service. Even to this day, I can recall how petrified with fear I was.

One fall evening I was at home alone. My mother had just gone to the store for a loaf of bread for supper. Suddenly, there was a loud, persistent pounding on the door. I opened it cautiously only to be greeted by a wild, disheveled-looking character, the likes of whom weren't seen too often in those days. He had a mop of curly black hair that curled over the collar of his ragged mackinaw. I will never forget him! His eyes! How I remember his cold, steely-blue eyes! They stabbed right through me and I was paralyzed with fright. I sensed something evil and sinister about him. Looking at me with a penetrating stare, he snapped in a menacing tone, "Is your father home?" Quaking in my shoes and wondering what he was about to do, I replied that my father would not be home until later on. Just as he turned to leave, the telephone started ringing off the hook. As I answered in a quivering voice, the excited one of a neighbor asked, "Lyla, is your father there, or your mother?" I again replied that my father would be home later on and that my mother had gone to the store and would return any minute. He hung up seeming quite perturbed and I wondered why.

On her way home from the store, my mother had to pass this neighbor's house and he stopped her as she went by. "Zettie," he said, "where's Lyle? I know he isn't home, but I wanted to warn him. Bill Peters* just stopped by here and said he was on his way to shoot that damned game warden, Lyle Smith, for arresting him for poaching deer last week. He meant business, I'm sure, as he was hiding a pistol under his coat. He will hold a grudge until his dying day as he never forgives or forgets. He was some wild and I was concerned."

Later, when my mother related this to my father, he scoffed and said he wasn't worried. Bill liked to put on a big act and besides, he was one of the biggest poachers on Mount Desert Island and Lyle was glad he had finally caught up with him. He could never convince me that the man was putting on an act. I was scared out of my wits, and to my dying day, I shall never forget that man's expression or the look in those awful eyes. He never bothered my father again, having probably cooled down when he didn't find him at home. I'm sure glad he wasn't there!

*Not his real name.

5

Besides the jacking of deer, the one thing that enraged Lyle beyond all else was dogs chasing deer. Death is ruthlessly violent and brutal once the dog has pulled the animal down. During late winter when we have thawing days and freezing nights come opportune times for dogs to chase deer. There is usually a crust formed on the snow due to the freezing and thawing which allows a dog to run on top of the crust without breaking through, while a deer, with its sharp hooves and heavier weight, will break through. The deer tire very quickly and are at the mercy of the dogs. Because pregnant does are most vulnerable, many are destroyed by dogs in late winter and early spring. Sometimes when a deer is chased onto an ice-covered lake or pond, the deer will spread-eagle on the ice and be unable to get up, making it very easy for dogs to subdue it. Dogs start to tear a deer apart while it is still living by pulling out vital organs to incapacitate the animal.

I recall the first time Lyle encountered such a sight. He was checking the carriage road which encircles Eagle Lake when he heard that intermittent, shrill barking of dogs which is unmistakably the sound of dogs on the trail of a deer. As he came around a sharp bend in the road a horrible sight met his eyes. Two large dogs had pulled down a ten-point buck and were literally tearing his innards out as the big animal bleated in pain and terror. His hindquarters were paralyzed and he was trying to escape by dragging himself along with his forelegs. With dead aim Lyle shot the two dogs and then destroyed the poor buck. I so well remember him relating the story to the family that evening, tears rolling down his cheeks as he spoke. I think the memory of this incident made him over-zealous in his pursuit of dogs killing deer. I know he destroyed many dogs caught in the act. As badly as he hated killing any living creature, I think shooting a "deer dog" was one deed he relished, especially when he caught them red-handed.

Lyle with dogs he killed after they had pulled down a doe. Dog in foreground is Mickey, our neighbor's friendly, three-legged pet. Dogs frequently chased deer onto the ice where they then became easy prey.

Once a dog learns to chase deer there is no breaking the habit. The minute he gets the chance he will head for the woods and the chase. Most dogs will chase a deer for a few feet until it gets out of sight, but a real "deer dog" acquires the lust for it by being with a dog that is already experienced. He will keep on the trail with a stubborn determination and ultimately a deer will be killed. Very few escape. The main reason for such a strict leash law throughout the state of Maine is because of this great damage to the deer herds. The law has helped somewhat but dog owners still need to be made more aware of what beasts their faithful, tail-wagging, ever-loving pets can become once addicted to chasing deer. Many pet owners would never believe it unless they see it with their own eyes.

Another advantage for dogs chasing deer is snowmobile tracks and trails through the woods. Many of these trails go further into the woods than a dog could naturally travel in deep snow. They skirt in and around deer yards and pack down the snow, which again makes it easier for the dogs to run and penetrate deeper into the forests.

An incident I recall involved a neighbor's friendly, gregarious, homely mongrel, who looked like a pit bull. He was good-natured, however. His name was Mickey and despite the fact that he had only three good legs, he could manipulate those three as well as most dogs could four. He had been struck by a car in his puppy days, injuring one hind leg. He was so protective of me that if a hand were laid on me for any reason, he would growl and get ready to attack. He grabbed a friend by the seat of the pants when the friend put his arm across my shoulders in a friendly gesture, and did not release his hold until I spoke to him. Every morning, religiously, Mickey escorted me to the school bus and waited patiently beside me until I was aboard.

One late winter afternoon, Lyle was snowshoeing down the eastern side of Western Mountain, again looking for deer dogs. About halfway down the trail he heard that familiar bark. In his excitement and haste to reach the lake below, from where the sound was coming, he skidded on the ice and crust just missing going over the side of the mountain. All that saved him was his belt which caught on a bush, holding him until he could get his snowshoes off and get back up onto the trail. He was battered a bit from the fall, but eventually got back on his feet. About half a mile away he saw the dogs. They already had a deer down on the ice and were ripping and tearing away in a wild and bloody frenzy. Snowshoe-fitted feet covering the distance in record time, he dispatched both dogs with the first two shots from his pistol. As he approached the bloody scene he quickly put the poor, pregnant doe out of her misery. But lo and behold, one of the dogs was our lovable little neighbor dog, Mickey. He was over ten miles from home and I wondered how his three, short, stubby legs had carried him on such a rigorous chase. As much as we loved him, no one shed a tear over his tragic demise. No, not even his master.

6

Although Lyle was a man of the earth and as much at home in the "forest primeval" as any creature of Mother Nature's realm, he was also a man of the twentieth century. He was twenty-five years ahead of his time in his thinking and ideas. He understood how and why man *had* to explore all the mysteries of the universe and the perplexing problems still unsolved. I'm sure if he had been fortunate enough to have received a formal education, unlimited horizons would have been opened up to him.

I remember when the comic strip *Flash Gordon* was first published. We children laughed because we were sure that no human could ever be propelled into space or walk on the moon or planets as Flash's adventures portrayed. My father sat in his easy chair perusing his paper and listening to our discussion. Finally, lowering his paper and with his "wise owl" look over the top of his reading glasses, he said, "Now you kids mark my words. Before you die, you will see a man walk on the moon."

We howled with laughter. I have always regretted that he didn't live long enough to see how right he was, and I would have gladly eaten humble pie in apologizing to him.

He could make anything he set his mind to and we children never worried over a broken toy, because Daddy could always fix it. He was endowed with great perseverance and ingenuity.

I remember when I was about four years old, he decided to go into the snowshoe business. There was no one around to teach him how to web snowshoes, so he studied a pair that he owned until he understood how they were woven. He then set up his workshop in the barn with the steam pipes and all the necessary equipment he would need to shape the frames. The previous year he had felled a big ash tree and had it milled and dried in preparation for his fledgling attempt at business. From somewhere he got deerhide already tanned and cut into narrow strips. When he had completed the frames, the difficult part started. Night after night, he sat in the kitchen with a pailful of wet deerhide beside his chair working on the webbing. At last he succeeded! The first pair was for me and what beauties they were! They were about three feet long with hand-made leather harnesses. How proud I was! I was the only kid around with a pair of tailor-made snowshoes, or any snowshoes for that matter. I could hardly contain myself and it didn't take long to master the art of using them. Before I knew it, I could go like the wind. I ran away so much that winter that my mother had to pin a note to my back to let neighbors and relatives know that I had her permission to visit.

Lyle sold all the snowshoes he could make for ten dollars a pair, a good price in those days. He by no means got very rich, for it was slow and tedious work. That enterprise lasted only one winter, but those who acquired his snowshoes would never part with them. I am still using a pair that he made for my mother over sixty-five years ago, and my children used the pair Lyle made for me. Today they are hanging over the mantel in my son's family room.

The greatest dream of Lyle's life was to fly an airplane. From the time I was a toddler in square pants, I recall his love of flying. How he would love to have his own plane! He regaled us with tales of air battles of World War I. The *Lafayette Escadrille, Sopwith Camel* or

German *Fokker* were not unfamiliar names to our young ears. He was forever creating toys that would eventually, through one process or another, be airborne.

Since insufficient income and seven mouths to feed prevented him from furthering his dream, he came up with another idea, which was not at all surprising from a man with his creative mind.

He was a hardy soul at best, but in winter when he had to check ice fishermen, he walked miles over snow-covered, frozen lakes. Those were the days before snowmobiles, and a warden's life was a rugged one in winter.

There were many ice fishermen on the numerous lakes of Mount Desert during ice-fishing season, and it was a day's work just to partly patrol and check Long Pond, the largest one. This is not only a large lake, but penetrating winter winds sweep across it with a vengeance. Despite his great stamina and the various accoutrements my mother designed for him to wear inside his wool long johns to protect sensitive-to-cold appendages, he was still chilled to the marrow of his bones at day's end. He said he was sick and tired of "freezing his butt off" every winter while checking fishermen and he was going to do something about it. Already, (and I suspect for some time) he had ideas formulating in his head.

One day he showed up with a trailer loaded with the blackened steel frame of a small airplane. My mother, who was nearly always prepared for most things unusual from my father, met him at the door with a look of exasperation and bewilderment on her usually smiling face. "Now whatever are you going to do with that old hunk of burned metal, Lyle Smith?"

"Well, a fellow over in Hancock sold this to me for fifteen dollars. His plane caught fire and burned but the frame's still good. I'm going to make myself an iceplane. If I cut the wingspan down and re-cover it, it'll be good as new. I don't want it to fly, I only want it to take me

Lyle with his non-flying iceplane. He built the plane to facilitate travel on frozen lakes during his frequent checks on ice fishermen.

around Long Pond when I check ice fishermen. It will need a motor but I'll find one somewhere around. It's a lot of work, but I have patience."

My poor mother turned away in despair. How did that man think he was going to build that contraption without it costing more money than they could really afford?

All the next year Lyle was obsessed with his iceplane. Every spare minute and penny went into it and he worked way into the night. It began to look like a smaller version of *The Spirit of St. Louis.* People from near and far came to see "Lyle's iceplane." He was so proud of it and could hardly wait for the day of takeoff.

My mother, concluding that boys will be boys, sputtered a bit about the five hundred dollars it cost to construct the thing, which then was a veritable fortune, but I think she was secretly pleased and proud, nevertheless.

Finally, open season on ice fishing arrived and the big day was upon us. It was a beautiful, crisp winter Sunday when the takeoff took place. The previous day, Lyle had hauled the plane sans wings to Long Pond where they had to be mounted in place. Due to their width the contraption was too wide to haul over the highway intact. By Saturday night it stood ready and awaiting its debut.

On Sunday afternoon people started gathering at the lake to watch the takeoff. A ripple of anticipatory excitement ran through the crowd. Soon, Lyle in his old Model A Ford came bumping along the rough woods road leading to the lake. Horn blaring like a bugle leading a charge to battle he came! The mob lining the shore cheered as he jumped out dressed in breeches, high boots, leather jacket, helmet, goggles, and, last but not least, a white silk scarf knotted around his neck. I'm sure that at that moment he felt a kinship with Charles Lindbergh or maybe the Red Baron. He certainly could have played a second to Lindy, as they were both tall, lanky and handsome. Again, the spectators cheered. "Come on, Lyle! Let's see what she can do!"

He turned on the ignition, then gave the propeller a few manual turns. The motor sputtered several times, caught, then roared to life.

Jumping aboard, Lyle turned and saluted the crowd just like a celebrity, before he closed the cockpit door. A ham if ever there was one!

He revved up the motor as if relishing that sound of power; the propeller spun smoothly and he was off. The crowd yelled and waved wildly.

The craft had traveled only a few hundred feet when it started to lift off the ice. *It wasn't supposed to fly!* It went up and up until it was a good six or seven feet off the ice and seemed to be gaining altitude. My heart did a flip-flop! How would he ever get it back onto the ice?

He knew nothing about flying. Everyone held his breath! It looked as if Lyle would be flying high any minute. I expected to see a crumpled pile of wreckage, my father crushed and broken beneath it. Suddenly he cut the motor and the plane glided a few feet, then settled gradually back onto the ice, wigging and wagging from side to side. Whew! He taxied back up the lake as the crowd gathered around. He threw open the cockpit door, blue eyes sparkling. "That damned thing nearly took off skyward! It wasn't supposed to do *that!* Scared the livin' hell out o' me! Now I'll have to cut the wings down some more and put skis on her. They'll work better than wheels."

In about two weeks the iceplane was equipped with skis and minus another foot or two of wingspan. *Now* it worked! It was quite a sight to see a plane that never took off, skimming over the ice, but it served its purpose beautifully. Of course, now ice fishermen had plenty of warning to get rid of any fish caught over size or bag limit.

Lyle used his iceplane for a couple of winters and then an incident occurred that caused my mother to put her foot down *hard.*

There was a small log cabin at the southern end of Long Pond which was constructed by the Civilian Conservation Corps in the '30's for the use of wardens and park rangers. This was located about three miles from where the iceplane was tethered. Frequently, in winter, my father and mother, along with my mother's sister, Aunt Lucy, and her husband, Uncle Jim, would spend a weekend there. So one late March Saturday afternoon, they set out for the cabin. Lyle decided that since the ice could be getting thin, it would be safer to ferry the girls down in the iceplane rather than drive the car over the ice. Then he'd come back for Uncle Jim and the supplies.

So he took the girls to the cabin and then went back for Uncle Jim. The girls got the fire going, carried in wood and water, then waited. After more than an hour had passed and there was no sign of the boys, they concluded that something had gone awry, and went looking for them. (By that time in March, the wind and water currents can cause crevices of open water which can be mighty dangerous and almost invisible until too late.)

They spotted the iceplane about halfway up the lake in what seemed to be a strange position. Now when you have to travel nearly two and a half miles on foot to get to what could be a catastrophe and over glare ice at that, you are pretty near a state of nervous collapse by the time of arrival, believe me. So it was with Mom and Aunt Lucy. There was the iceplane, nose down, headed into a crevice, tail sticking up in the air. Lyle and Uncle Jim were pulling, pushing and prying with long poles they had cut, trying to get the thing upright again. All that had saved them from heading straight to Davy Jones's locker, if there is one in fresh water, was the propeller, which had stopped at just such an angle across the crevice that it kept the iceplane from going down.

Lyle, looking a bit sheepish as the girls approached, said, "Golly, I thought I could gun 'er across that crack but a ski caught and she nose-dived."

Finally they got the contraption righted and on its merry way. It wasn't long after that episode that Lyle's iceplane was for sale.

However, Lyle's dream of flying finally did come to fruition. When he was in his early fifties, just after World War II, he met a young pilot of considerable wealth. They struck up an immediate, close friendship. The young pilot, knowing Lyle's love of flying, one day said to him, "Pappy, if you can earn your pilot's license, I'll see that you have a plane of your own."

That really started the ball rolling! At once he enrolled for flying instruction at nearby Bar Harbor Airport, much to my mother's disapproval.

Just landed from a flight. Lyle with grandchildren, Bill and Jane St. Louis.

Lyle thought of nothing else but taking to the wild blue yonder. Then one day he soloed! That was a day to remember! I can see him now, tall, lanky figure unfolding from the cockpit, grinning from ear to ear, blue eyes shining. His friend, waiting anxiously, embraced him, then handed him the keys to a small red-and-white plane sitting on the runway. "You did it, Pappy! I knew you would and there she sits," he said, gesturing toward the little Aeronica Chief behind him. True to his word he was! Lyle's patience and determination had paid off.

For years he flew like a bird. Even my mother condescended to join him on flights, and she, too, found she loved flying as much as my father. He became known as the "Flying Warden," and then he really did fly over the frozen lakes to check the ice fishermen, only now he could take off and land to perfection in a real plane.

My father's experience goes to prove once again that if one has a life's dream and perseveres toward that end, it can become a reality. I have always admired his great determination and tenacity, and whenever I have needed a boost in spirit, I think of him and it has always helped.

The story of Lyle's iceplane is still a legend in these parts today.

A couple of years after Lyle retired from the Warden Service, his flying career came to an abrupt end.

One early March day he had tied the plane down on the shore of Somes Pond a couple of miles from home. That late afternoon a spring rain struck with warm gale-force winds accompanying it. Several times during the evening, Lyle checked to see how the plane was weathering the storm. He checked it last about midnight. All was fine and it looked as if she'd be secure for the rest of the night. She was in a protected area, so he thought, and he went back home not too worried over it.

Next morning bright and early, he checked again. No, his little plane hadn't moved an inch, but her fuselage was smashed to smithereens. An old rowboat which had been turned upside down on the shore some feet away had apparently become loosened from the ice by the warm wind and rain. When a high gust of wind struck, it lifted the rowboat up and rammed it right into the plane. A freak accident, as well as a heartbreaking one for Lyle. The damage was heavy and the insurance did not completely cover it, so he decided to sell the plane for what it was worth. It had become quite an expense to maintain, anyway, on a retired warden's pay back in those days. He had a ball while it lasted, to say the least, as well as having a life's dream accomplished.

7

Probably the most poignant episode of Lyle's warden career, both for the public and our family, resulted from the rescue of a baby fawn.

She came into our lives one early June day in 1942. A mite of a thing she was, so delicate and fragile. Her head, finely chiseled, held large dark eyes that loomed too large for such a tiny face and peered out at us with deep, questioning wonder. Her ears, also, were large and looked overgrown on her minute head. Her coat, a warm reddish shade of tan, was interspersed with camouflage spots of pure white that sloped softly away to the all-white of her underbelly. Her little flag waved almost constantly, back and forth, when she trotted about, as if she were warning the animal kingdon to beware of these strange, two-legged creatures who now held her captive.

Since she was almost newborn, her dainty hoofs looked as if they had been carved from old ivory as they had not yet matured enough to turn black. Her thin, spindly legs propelled her about in a very wobbly fashion. Occasionally she would attempt to run, and end up flat on her face wearing a most bewildered expression as she scrambled back on her feet. We thought she was less than two days old.

She soon adapted to her new surroundings and became very trusting. She had been rescued by two hikers, near a trail in Acadia National Park. The mother had been killed by dogs that very day and the hikers happened upon her remains. The fawn, no doubt, being hungry and sensing the full impact of her loss, was stumbling about on her wobbly legs and bleating piteously for her mother. The hikers sized up the situation at once, realizing the poor little thing could not survive without help and brought her to my father.

Within a couple of days our little orphan had melded into our home and routine as if she had been born and bred in the very heart of civilization. We decided to name her Bambi after the deer in Walt Disney's movie, which was very popular at that time. However, our Bambi was a doe and Disney's a buck.

Lyla and Bambi.

Bambi needed as much care and attention as a newborn babe. She required a special formula and there always had to be those extra bottles in the refrigerator to warm whenever she was hungry. When this happened, she would inevitably seek out some member of the family, usually my mother, who bore the brunt of her care. If Mom were sitting down, Bambi would put her forefeet in Mom's lap and suck on her nearest ear lobe. It was always a sign she wanted her bottle. As she grew older and became weaned, she continued to do this to those people she loved. It seemed to become a gesture of affection and we called it an "ear kiss." It was really comical to watch, especially when she became a full-grown doe. By that time she could reach the average ear without standing on her hind legs. Lyle was probably the only exception, since he was over six feet tall. How she loved him! He seemed to have a special affinity for God's creatures and they sensed it. I recall the time a poor old skunk crossed the road in front of the car, a salmon can caught over his head. My father stopped the car, picked up the skunk who had been groping blindly about, and removed the can. The skunk cast him a grateful look as he loped away into the bushes without further ado. We thought our father was so courageous to do that. This quality, I think, made him such a good warden. He told us that a wild animal usually senses when it is being helped by a human, normally its greatest enemy.

All summer our yard was thronged with visitors, especially on weekends. Bambi was a curiosity and loved all the attention, but it was hard on my mother as she was constantly answering the door. Bambi was allowed to roam free, and my mother would call her by blowing a whistle. Visitors stood speechless as she came bounding out of the woods and across the field, going directly to my mother and giving her an ear kiss. Next, she greeted each visitor by sniffing them from head to toe. The more she liked the smell, the longer her investigation. She liked people who smoked most of all, and if she could ferret out a pack of cigarettes, she'd try her best to get at them. We had to watch her constantly around ashtrays as she would gobble up those butts and lick the trays clean. We could never figure out her fondness for tobacco, but I suspect it could affect animals just as it does humans.

As Bambi's first summer passed, she completely adjusted to a civilized life. She went wherever she pleased, but usually stayed in the house at night. Dogs were our greatest concern, so we kept a watchful eye on her. The dogs in the neighborhood were afraid of her as she would strike out at them with her sharp hoofs and send them reeling end over end. This happened a few times and from that time on they didn't bother her. It was the strange dogs we worried about. Once when she was outside and no one was at home, some dogs did chase her, and she jumped right through the living room window. When my father and mother returned home she was watching them from the kitchen window. Surprised, my mother said, "Lyle, I thought you put that deer outside when we left?"

My father, also looking surprised, replied, "I sure did, and the kids haven't come home from school yet to let her in." Upon investigation they found dog tracks in the late spring snow that led right up to the window. Probably the only reason the dogs didn't go in after her was because they couldn't jump high enough to get through the window. In any event, she knew where she'd be safe.

By the time Bambi was a year old she had become a well-known attraction throughout the state, as well as points north, south, east and west. Nationally-read newspapers had published articles about her with accompanying pictures. Photographers were frequent visitors. She was loved by all the neighborhood children, and went with them on hikes and skating parties, and even rode the school bus each day. The local general

Two of Bambi's favorite things: riding the school bus and getting her daily handout at the general store.

store owner always had a handout ready for her and a visit was a part of her morning ritual. It wasn't unusual to see her trotting up the street on her way to the store to collect.

There were certain neighbors she made routine visits to as well. One usually had a doughnut to give; another would have a cookie, and another a carrot. She would stand on the steps looking in the window, ears pricked forward, watching for an indication that she was about to be let in. Once she stole a lady's cookie dough when the woman left her door open.

One night there was a cowboy show in the local grange hall. Bambi always attended all community functions held there, walking up and down the aisles to greet her friends with an ear kiss. This particular night as the music started she left abruptly. I guess it must have been too much for her sensitive ears. As she came out of the hall, a stranger drove by and saw her. He did a double take! Immediately, he stopped at the general store to inquire. Excitedly, he said to the clerk, "I know I'm not drunk and I didn't think I was crazy, but I just saw a big doe deer coming out of that hall across the street!"

The clerk went on to explain that he had no cause for worry and then told him the story of Bambi. Relieved, the stranger proceeded on his way.

When Bambi was a year and a half old, and the mating season approached, we hoped that she would join her own kind and take to the wilds. She was now old enough to produce a fawn come spring, and we all looked forward to it. She had suddenly taken to going farther afield and frequently ended up in Trenton on the mainland, where there was an open season on deer hunting. People were constantly calling my father to say that Bambi was at their door or in a nearby field, so Lyle would drive over to pick her up in the car. She would ride in the back seat, her head sticking out of the open window just as a dog would. Hunters had a quizzical expression on their faces when they saw Lyle driving by with her. As I've heretofore mentioned, there is a perpetual closed season on deer hunting on Mount Desert Island, so we thought she was safe, little dreaming that she would trot right across the bridge to the mainland over three miles away. Little did we know what lay in store either. My mother decided to make her a red jacket, much like a wide harness, and decorated with large gold buttons. No hunter could mistake a deer wearing that for a wild deer. My sister even painted Bambi's hoofs with bright red nail polish as an added protection. She sure looked comical wearing that jacket, but it didn't bother her in the least.

In late October the tragedy which cast a pall over our family and our community occurred. A poacher shot and killed Bambi a few yards from our house, in the pasture lane. My father found her remains tied up and buried under leaves and brush, as if hidden until it would be safe to come back for her. With tears streaming down his face, he broke the news to the family. Wardens and state police descended upon the scene, but all the evidence they could find was an empty 10-gauge shotgun shell. It was never proven for sure who had killed her. Lyle suspected a neighbor who owned a 10-gauge but he gave Lyle a big run-around. Later on, his house burned and the barrel of a 10-gauge was found, but the breech was lost, so there was no way of matching the gun to the bullet that was found. In later years, a close relative of this neighbor told me that the man had not killed Bambi. He said he knew who did, and named the man who had appeared at our door that frightening night when I was a child, with the intention of shooting my father. When I have thought about this over the years, I wonder if it was done out of revenge. This man never forgot or forgave, but he, along with the suspected neighbor and my father, have long since gone to their Maker.

As for Bambi, she had a wonderful year and a half of life that would never have been possible if she had not

Lyle and Bambi.

been rescued by the hikers. She, no doubt, would have suffered the same fate as her mother.

As for my family, we were grateful that we had shared in the experiences and adventures of a wild creature, and our life with Bambi served to make us appreciate even more than before the gift of wildlife that God has bestowed upon us. Bambi reminded us that we should, each and every one of us, do all within our power to conserve and preserve wild things for future generations. My father's words will forever echo through my mind: "We must protect and conserve our wildlife if we want it to go on forever."

8

I could never in good conscience tell this story without paying deep tribute to my mother, who, besides raising five active children, did all within her power to ease the burden of my father's work. There were days, as well as numerous nights, that the doorbell and telephone rang with a never-ending clamor. Someone was always in need of blood meal to keep the deer out of his garden, a trapper needed a license application, or he just had to see the game warden. No matter what the problem, the fact was that she was constantly pulled away from her housework. I still marvel at how she put such wonderful meals on the table, cooked scrumptious cakes, pies and doughnuts, milked cows, raised pigs and chickens, and churned her own butter. As each winter approached, the cellar was full of canned foods, jams, pickles and mincemeat, to name just a few. In addition to everything else, she was very active in the affairs of our small community.

There was little that fazed her in the way of warden's duties, either. Occasionally, she had to cut a deer's throat after it had been struck and killed by a car and brought to our house. If Lyle were away, she'd do it, though it wasn't exactly to her liking. In any event, it was the lesser of two evils as the meat would be ruined if the deer wasn't bled. As previously stated, unless the person who struck the deer wanted to take it as compensation for damages to his car, it was delivered to nursing

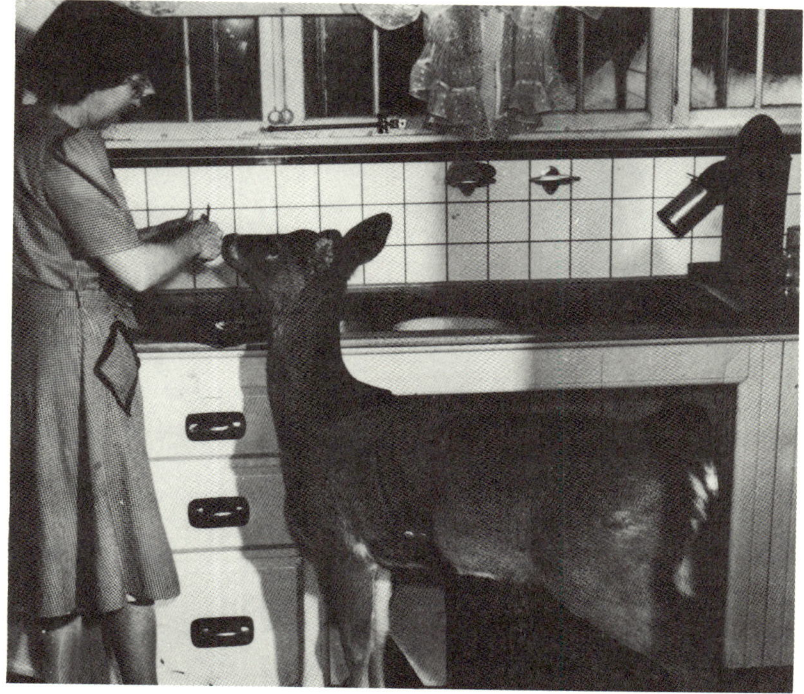

Waiting for the peelings as Mom pares the potatoes.

homes and to needy families. The job of butchering usually fell to Lyle.

There were often extra people for meals and that didn't seem to bother her one iota. We had a huge oval oak dining room table and a place or two extra was easily accommodated. During duck-hunting season the hunters descended upon us en masse, it seemed. To begin with, many of them were well-known sportsmen connected with various newspapers and publications. Lyle was always ready to talk to them and to escort them to the best duck-hunting grounds. It became a yearly ritual for several of them to come to our house for one of my mother's delectable duck dinners. She was an excellent wild game cook and had achieved quite a reputation among sportsmen for her coot stew. She prepared this in such a way that it would appeal to the palate of the most fastidious gourmet. I've heard old time duck hunters say jokingly that to prepare coot you should put it into a large kettle with a big rock. Add plenty of onions, salt, pepper and water. Cook for twelve hours, then throw out the coot and eat the rock. She amazed many a hunter when they tasted this dish. They used to say, "You haven't tasted anything until you've tasted Zettie Smith's coot stew!" They were flabbergasted that it could be so delicious and said they wished they had known how to prepare the birds long ago. They felt guilty when they thought of all the coot they'd discarded. They just couldn't seem to get rid of that strong, fishy taste that was prevalent in coot. I think her secret was that she soaked them in salt and water for at least twenty-four hours.

The house buzzed with never-ending activity of the sort which revolved around my father's work, and since he was away a great deal, all the extra responsibilities came to rest upon my mother's shoulders. I don't recall her ever complaining about all the work she had to do. She had a happy, sunny disposition and was ever ready to lend a helping hand to man or beast. Countless injured and orphaned animals she nursed back to health, which required much time and effort along with so many interruptions. By the same token, sick and needy neighbors were always looked out for by her whenever she knew they needed help. To this very day I am still awestruck at her patience, endurance and fortitude.

During The Great Bar Harbor Fire of 1947, my mother directed one of the canteens set up for the fire-fighters, which was in operation twenty-four hours a day. When the fire was at its worst, she was unable to go home even for a brief forty winks. One morning about 3:00, she managed to get a couple of free hours so she could go home, take a bath, change her clothes and catch a bit of sleep. She had to walk about a quarter of a mile home and when nearly there she came unexpectedly upon a poor, bewildered skunk. Because the pall of smoke hung thick and low over the early morning landscape, she spied him too late. He was in no way particular to whom he displayed partiality. In all the chaos everything was his enemy. He let her have it! Being so near to him, the spray covered her, nearly blinding and choking her to death. When she reached the house, she disrobed outside, and by the time she had gotten cleaned up, it was time to be back on duty. No shut-eye that night!

Later, we all sympathized with her, but she said our sympathy should lie with the poor skunk. He was so bedazzled and befuddled by the fire, smoke and commotion, that he shouldn't be blamed for trying to protect himself. All the animals trying to escape the inferno were in a state of fright and frenzy.

An incident I recall between my mother and father that struck me in a humorous way occurred the day after the attack on Pearl Harbor when President Roosevelt formally declared war against Japan and Germany.

At the time Lyle was forty-seven years old and a more devout and loyal patriot had never walked this earth. After listening to the President's ominous words, Lyle turned to Zettie with the most serious expression on his face, his voice cracking with emotion. "I'm going to Bangor and enlist in the navy right now!"

My mother looked at him aghast for a moment, replying disgustedly, "For God's sake, you know you can't do that!"

"Well, I don't know why I can't. I was a darned good sailor in World War I and I can do it again. This country needs good men. Bad!"

"You might be a good man, Lyle Smith, but don't you realize you're too damned old?"

That speech coming from my mother who never used a curse word really struck me funny, and stopped

Lyle dead in his tracks. Yes, he was too old in years but certainly not in spirit. He threw himself wholeheartedly into the war effort doing whatever our country called upon its civilian population to do and then some.

One night as Lyle was hurrying to Ellsworth to meet Raymond Morse, his supervisor, the tables were turned on him. (Morse headed Division F, District 31, of the Warden Service.)

It was the last weekend of November and the end of deer-hunting season was approaching. Raymond had instructed all his wardens to meet him at his home in Ellsworth as they were setting up roadblocks along Route One to check illegal transportation of game. This weekend would be the climax of the season when out-of-state hunters would be leaving.

The men were to meet at 7:00 P.M. and then proceed from there. This was the time of year when wardens put in extra long hours. Lyle had been working eighteen to twenty hours a day and was exhausted, so he decided he would catch a few minutes of sleep before it was time to leave. He cautioned my mother to be sure to wake him at 6:00 P.M. so he would have plenty of time to get there. This she did, and then immediately left to attend a meeting, thinking he would be on his way. He fell asleep again and when he awoke it was well past 7:00 P.M. Decidedly flustered and upset, he made a mad dash for Ellsworth. By the time it had begun to snow hard and visibility was poor. He had gotten nearly halfway there when a big doe jumped from the side of the road, smashing the fender and denting the hood of the car, doing considerable damage. Luckily, the car was still operable. The poor doe had to be destroyed, she was so badly injured. There was nothing to do but load the deer onto the car and proceed on his way. By the time he got to Ray's house, the wardens had all departed to set up the roadblock, leaving a message for Lyle as to where they would be. There was a bit of kidding going on that night, you can rest assured. I remember well the damage to the car was $150. By today's prices it would probably be $2,500. When Zettie was told about the accident, she replied, "You know, Lyle, haste always makes waste." So typical of her.

When I was a teenager and began to realize what my mother's assistance, concern and solicitude meant to my father, and the infinite sacrifices she had made, I wrote the following poem. George J. Stobie, who was still Commissioner of Inland Fisheries and Game, had it framed and hung on the wall of his office in the State House in Augusta.

THE GAME WARDEN'S WIFE

Some people think a warden's life
Is an easy, carefree one,
But what about the warden's wife,
Do you think she has fun?

She works each day from dawn till dark,
Her work is never done,
She goes upstairs to make the beds,
Ding ling! The doorbell's rung.

She hurries quickly down the stairs,
And rushes to the door.
"Is the warden in?" a stranger asks.
"No, he won't be in till four."

Then back she goes about her work.
She starts to bake a cake.
The telephone rings ding-a-ling.
"No, he won't be home till late."

The whole day long she's back and forth
From door to telephone.
I wonder how she carries on
The spirit of home sweet home.

She spends the frosty nights alone,
But soon gets used to that.
At least she doesn't have to have
Those cold feet in her back!

She's up all hours of the night.
She's lost all trace of fear.
A stranger standing at the door
Says, "My car's just struck a deer."

"Did you cut its throat?" she promptly asks,
Then grabs the butcher knife.
"If you haven't, I can do that, too.
It's nothing in my life."

So if you think a warden's wife
Can live a life that's grand,
Just change with her a day or two,
And then you'll understand.

9

After serving twenty-five years in the Warden Service, Lyle decided to retire. He had suffered a severe heart attack that last year from which he was nearly six months recovering. He was now fifty-seven years old and he said if he lived to be a hundred, he would never have enough time left to do all the things he had planned.

That fall of 1953, he and the Service parted company. He then took a part-time job as a researcher with the Fisheries Research Division of the Maine Department of Inland Fisheries and Game. Their basic goal was to find ways to improve the fishing in Maine's inland lakes and streams. Lyle's duties mostly involved taking creel checks at streams and lakes on the island, interviewing fishermen about their catches and weighing and measuring the fish. This work required only a few hours a week, and supplemented the meager state pension he received at that time, which I recall was in the area of $125 a month.

An investment he had made just before World War II was a parcel of land on Long Pond, which he hoped would some day be valuable. How foresighted he was! The plot contained almost two acres with a considerable stretch of shore frontage. On it was situated an old building which had at one time been used as a fishing camp. It was still structurally sound and he used it mainly to store fishing and boating gear. The property lay at the head of the lake, overlooking a scene of breathtaking beauty that encompassed a spread of azure blue water in the foreground and swept away to a backdrop of purple mountains. He loved this spot and in 1947, he, along with my brother Bob and my mother, established a small seasonal restaurant there, aptly named Pond's End, although he was unable to help out to any extent until he retired.

Throughout his warden's career, Lyle had rubbed noses with many of this country's rich and famous. We children were unimpressed when a chauffeured limousine drove into our yard and a richly uniformed chauffeur stepped out asking for our father. When I look back upon those days, I realize what an era I was raised

Lyle and his plane, at retirement on October 30, 1953.
Photo-BANGOR DAILY NEWS

in. Today, around Mount Desert Island, such gorgeous automobiles driven by extravagantly liveried chauffeurs are rarely, if ever, seen. After World War II, they disappeared with the changing times.

During the 1940's, Charles Wilson, who was Secretary of Defense under President Eisenhower, came to the house to enjoy a wild duck dinner. Lyle had escorted him on several duck-hunting excursions and he was overjoyed with the results. When my mother prepared one of her delicious meals of wild duck, he was beyond himself with this delicacy prepared as only she knew how.

Another famous visitor was Joseph Pulitzer, Jr. of the *St. Louis Post Dispatch*. Mr. Pulitzer's wife loved duck hunting and my father escorted them on many a hunting expedition. He even built a duck blind for them at the shore.

One early morning when the ducks were really flying in, and the Pulitzers had already acquired their bag-limit, Mrs. Pulitzer excitedly turned to Lyle and asked, "Lyle, if you could have anything you wished for at this moment, what would it be?"

"Well," replied Lyle, off the top of his head, "I guess I'd wish for a 12-gauge Remington automatic shotgun." He gave it no further thought until the next day. That morning the Pulitzers showed up with the wished-for gift, much to Lyle's surprise. He cherished that shotgun until his dying day, though I doubt that he ever used it very much. It hung in a place of honor over the fireplace in his den until his death and now belongs to my brother, Leslie.

A colorful personality with whom Lyle became friends in his early warden years was Needabeh, Chief of the Penobscots. I first saw Needabeh when I was about thirteen, and Lyle was the official greeter at a field day being sponsored by the Mount Desert Island Fish and Game Association at the southern end of Long Pond, with several state officials in attendance. Needabeh was the featured guest and was to give a fly-fishing exhibition. He appeared there in his colorful chief's regalia with the long headdress of eagle's feathers streaming down his back. He was striking in appearance—majestic—almost to the point of being overpowering. I was highly impressed to see a real Indian chief. The high point of that day for me was having my first airplane ride. This was in the Fish and Game Department's plane which had flown the state officials in. *And* I got to sit beside Needabeh! The thrill of a lifetime for a thirteen-year-old!

Eventually, Lyle and Needabeh became arch competitors in fly-fishing competitions. Needabeh was an accomplished fly fisherman and Lyle was no novice at it, either. At fish and game field day events and shows throughout the state, the two of them would compete. Several times Lyle won these events against Needabeh and that was great cause for celebration.

Another famous personage with whom he established a fine friendship was Mary Roberts Rinehart, the well-known writer of mysteries, who owned a lovely estate in Bar Harbor, high on a hill overlooking Frenchman Bay. Her mansion was destroyed in The Great Fire of 1947, and today, in its place, stands a popular motel and restaurant. Two or three times each summer, during her stay in Bar Harbor, Mrs. Rinehart would phone Lyle to come for afternoon tea. She loved to discuss the politics of the island and to learn about the conservation and preservation of its resources. Inevitably, he left with a bottle of the finest Scotch under his arm. She was a lovely, down-to-earth lady and interested in all aspects of Mount Desert Island's life.

After The Great Fire of 1947, the men of our little community, under Lyle's supervision, joined together to form the Town Hill Fire Department. Lyle was elected fire chief, a position that he held for many years. This was strictly a volunteer fire company to which all its members were highly dedicated. Here again, Lyle took his position as chief as seriously and with as much dedi-

Trucks of the Town Hill Fire Department, which Lyle worked diligently to establish after The Great Bar Harbor Fire in 1947. The Department has proved its worth many times over.

cation as he did his warden's duties. He had seen firsthand so much devastation in the '47 fire, before which men stood helpless, that he would do all within his power to help prevent another such holocaust. He organized beano games, card parties, suppers and turkey shoots, as well as raffles, to raise money for a fire truck. Finally, their goal reached, Lyle and the assistant chief, Benny Gilbert, traveled to Worcester, Massachusetts, to pick up the new truck. That small group of men had raised nearly $5,000 in about a year to purchase it. In those days, a new car cost about $1,000, so raising that much money was a great undertaking for a small community organization. The Town Hill Fire Department has proven its worth many times over during the past years.

Lyle had creative and organizational talents in many other areas, as well. Once he had made up his mind to do something, he could not rest until it was done. Both he and my mother were active members of Mt. View Grange, Patrons of Husbandry. Whenever a fund-raising project was to be launched, both of them were right in the thick of it. In the late '30's, Lyle conceived a plan to put on a circus to raise money for the grange. All the people in the community were involved in it, from babes-in-arms to the very old. It turned out to be a mammoth undertaking. Lyle was expected to be the director of operations and design, so to speak, since the circus idea was his brain child. It took all winter and spring to organize and prepare for it. The ladies of the grange, under my mother's tutelage, met at our house to sew costumes, which were most colorful and elegant. My sister, Harriet, was the trapeze artist and I can still see her flying through the air on a trapeze suspended from the grange hall ceiling. Lyle left no stone unturned!

Lyle and his crew built bleachers around the main floor of the hall, the center of the hall being the ring for the show. He constructed giraffes and elephants from wire frames covered with cloth and then painted them. Each animal was life-size and large enough to accomodate two adults inside, one in front and one in back. The ears, tails, mouths, trunks, etc. were all workable from inside. They really looked alive! Lyle trained the operators in how to walk and act like the real animals. I can still see him giving them instructions. He himself was a clown in the show, and brought the house down with his shenanigans. He made a gorilla costume from a dark brown bull's hide that he got from Cappy Lunt, the local dairyman. Benny Gilbert, who could imitate the walk and gait of a gorilla to perfection, was chosen for this part. Lyle had Benny lie down on the bullhide and with a piece of chalk, traced around him to get the costume the right size. He sewed every inch of that hide by hand using an awl to puncture it before he could insert a needle. No easy task! The head of papier-mâché, acquired from a costume supply house, looked lifelike. Lyle had constructed the costume so that a hood came up over the head, making the creature look so true-to-life that when Benny came sauntering into the circus ring, the adults let out a cry of disbelief and the kids, frightened out of their wits, screamed and howled at the top of their lungs. He made a frightening appearance! Amid all this pandemonium Benny thrived. He rode a tricycle around the ring, occasionally letting out a blood-curdling roar which shook the rafters. I could go on and on telling the tales of Hi Jink's Circus, which was a raving success. Today, over fifty years later, it is still talked and reminisced about. The troupe was sought after constantly to put on the show in Bangor, Augusta and other communities, but it would have taken a train the size of Ringling Brothers' to accomodate all the necessary people, props and animals. However, it played in the grange hall four succeeding nights, each time to a full house. With all the people in that old hall, it's a wonder the place didn't collapse.

The year the circus was presented I wrote the following poem which aptly describes some of the many and varied acts, and was used in advertising. Admission, by the way, was only fifty cents!

HI JINK'S CIRCUS

The animals and the clowns are here,
The same as every other year.
See Hi Jink's Circus, the biggest on earth,
You'll always get your money's worth.

There are the craziest clowns in all creation.
Why, they even perform an operation!
They laugh and sing and dance and holler,
Say, folks, this show is worth a dollar!

Then there's the bull called Ferdinand
And he is really very grand.
The elephants and the tall giraffe
Will make you all just laugh and laugh.

There's Waldo, the rooster, a very large bird.
The largest on earth, so far as I've heard.

We have a trained bear who knows how to box,
He fights with the clowns and gets a few knocks.

The cowgirls and cowboys and Indians, too,
Put on as good a show as you ever knew.
The dancers and skaters are certainly clever,
Why, this circus is bigger and better than ever!

And Toni O'Brien rides a pony bareback,
She's certainly cute dressed in silver and black.
And Dixie Carroll upon the trapeze
Glides back and forth with the greatest of ease.

The tightrope walker, named Donna Lee,
Is as pretty and sweet as she can be.
There's Shirley Temple from way out West
And she can dance the very best.

Jim and Joe, the world's largest twins,
With their big fat legs and double chins,
Surely are a funny sight,
Especially when they have a fight.

From the Far North comes our Eskimo,
Here from the land of ice and snow,
He has with him a bird that's tame,
He's black and white and "Kool's" his name.

There's crazy Sally and foolish Si,
If you could see 'em you'd surely die
A-laughin' at the things they do,
They're awfully funny let me tell you!

Then there's Otto, the gorilla,
Who looks ferocious but he's not a killer.
He rides a bike around the ring,
But I know he wouldn't hurt a thing.

There's a lady with a great long beard,
And no matter how many times it's sheared,
It always manages to grow,
So we hired her for this show.

Then Jocko, our monkey, as everyone knows,
Can hang by his tail and dance on his toes,
And we have a cannibal from way down South,
Who's got wooly hair and a great big red mouth.

From Borneo we have a man,
And he's the wildest in the land,

He'll screech and holler and try to fight,
Your blood will chill at his very sight.

Last, but not least, we mustn't forget
Samanthy Ann who's with us yet.
She's been with this circus for many a year,
We hope she won't leave us for she's an old dear.

We have all kinds of the freakiest freaks,
That any one of you would ever seek,
So don't miss this circus 'way up to Town Hill
For you'll certainly find you'll get a great thrill.

Now, if anyone happens to make fun of us,
You'll not hear any of us making a fuss,
We're not professionals, we know,
But after all, we're not so slow.

I mention these events merely to show that Lyle was a man of many talents with an innate sense of determination to accomplish whatever he set out to do.

10

After Lyle retired from the Warden Service in the fall of 1953, he had more time to devote to the work and activities at Pond's End each summer. This was a seasonal restaurant and extra help was always welcomed. As previously stated, my brother Bob had started the business in 1947, shortly after being mustered out of the army after World War II. He had had some restaurant experience and was an excellent chef. Before we realized what was happening, Pond's End became very popular and noted for its good food. Each year that old fishing camp was enlarged in some way, until it began to look like "The House That Jack Built." People came from near and far to savor Bob's delicious meals, which were prepared with the self-assured flourish of the gourmet and served in a rustic setting in which the elegant vied with the rudimentary. The dinner guests loved it when Bob dashed from the kitchen to the dining room between preparing orders and rattled off a song or two at the piano. He had a beautiful voice and singing was only one of his many talents. Occasionally, some of the help would don costumes and present a skit under Bob's direction or even a song or two. It was much like today's dinner theatre on a small scale, and everyone enjoyed it immensely.

With the growth in business, my mother, Zettie, took over the pastry cooking, which added to the popularity of the restaurant, particularly her home-made pies and doughnuts.

During the winter months, after Pond's End was opened, Lyle built rowboats to rent to fishermen. Each winter he built one or two more, which added up to quite a fleet. These boats proved to be a great convenience to fishermen and were much in demand.

The Bar Harbor fire in 1947 completely changed the face of Mount Desert Island. No longer was Bar Harbor to be a mecca for the wealthy and socially elite. It gradually became a highly popular tourist attraction, as did the whole island. With the war years behind us, people began to travel once again. They came from everywhere—this country and abroad. The natural beauty of Acadia National Park drew people like flies. Europeans, particularly, fell in love with its mountains, lakes and ocean. It was so much like the homeland many had been forced to leave behind during the war years.

Eventually, Pond's End became a meeting place for residents and summer residents alike. My family welcomed them all with open arms and each felt that Pond's End was a home away from home, with its warm hospitality and exceptional food. It became a focal point for the "back side of the island," as the local folks referred to the western part of Mount Desert. Messages were left here, keys to camps, mail, luggage, you name it, we had it.

In the late '50's, Bob, who had wintered in the Virgin Islands, decided to open a restaurant in St. Thomas and did not return to Pond's End that year. Lyle and Zettie continued to operate the business. Here again, Lyle with his strong, outgoing personality made an excellent host, and people loved to hear the tales he was always ready to tell to a listening ear. Some of the activities and goings-on that took place there are talked about today, with Lyle, as a rule, the main character.

After Lyle's death in 1961, Zettie ran the business through the summer of 1965. By that time, it had become too great a burden and responsibility for her, so she decided to close. A few years later, the old building,

A busy summer's day at Pond's End, which Lyle enjoyed in his retirement years.

which had begun to deteriorate badly, was torn down. She then sold the property to the State of Maine Department of Parks and Recreation. Lyle's hope had always been that the state would eventually acquire this property so the public would have access to one of Mount Desert's most beautiful lakes. There were no easily accessible boat-launching sites on the lake, and land was fervently being bought up privately. Also, during Lyle's warden years, he had been instrumental in establishing a seaplane base at Pond's End, which was designated on the map of Mount Desert Island. He himself had built plane ramps to accommodate seaplanes and during the early years the ramps were always occupied. Today, though it's not nearly as busy as in those early years, planes use it frequently. Now Pond's End is also a popular site for boaters, picnickers, and fishermen who are able to enjoy one of this island's loveliest spots. I'm sure that only a few are aware of the fact that Lyle and Zettie Smith were solely responsible for making this place available to the public.

Over the eighteen years that Lyle and Zettie owned and operated Pond's End, many wonderful and lasting friendships were made. Some of those friends have passed away, but many continue to come to the island. Because of their love for Pond's End, several have built summer homes up and down the lake. This was where they wanted to spend their vacations. The younger generation of those days is now grown with families of its own, and they continue to come back, too, remembering those wonderful times they had when Pond's End was in its heyday. They all reiterate the same words, "We'll never miss a place the way we miss Pond's End, and the great times we had there. No one can replace Lyle and Zettie."

Now Pond's End with its happy days has passed into the Great Beyond, as have my father, mother, and Bob. It was a time and place never to be forgotten by the many who knew and loved it. However, the site still stands as a never-to-be-forgotten memorial to the two people who made it possible, Lyle and Zettie Smith.

11

In the sixty-five years that Lyle was allotted on this earth, his achievements were many. First, he had a career which he loved and to which he was entirely dedicated, and that completely fulfilled him. Secondly, for a man in his financial position, he attained by sheer determination and effort luxuries which generally fell only to the very wealthy. He had learned to fly and had owned his own airplane when he was over fifty years old, and in the course of a few years, had owned two yachts. Not many working men of his era could match that. Also, he was a devoted friend and neighbor in the community, always willing to lend a helping hand, as well as being a beloved and highly respected law enforcement officer. To my knowledge, few people whom he had arrested because of an infraction of the fish and game laws ever resented it or held it against him. Only one am I able to recall. I have heard some of them say, "I knew I was breaking the law, and if Smitty caught me, it's my own fault. It's his job to enforce the law." *And* that he did!

Once when my husband, Tom, and I stopped to browse at the prison store in Thomaston, Tom began to talk with the prison trusty who was working in the store. The trusty asked him where we were going and Tom told him we were on our way back to Freeport from Bar Harbor.

The trusty, looking surprised, replied, "I'm from Northeast Harbor, right next door."

My husband said, "Well, we're practically neighbors. I married a Town Hill girl—Lyle Smith's daughter. Do you know him?"

"Know him!" retorted the trusty. "He's the guy who sent me up here."

I had remained in the car with the baby, so my husband invited him out to meet me. He shook my hand and said he was glad to meet me and told me he was well acquainted with my grandfather, grandmother and aunt and uncle who lived in Northeast Harbor. It seems he and a friend had killed a deer in the park area and hidden it in a trunk they had taken from a summer cottage. When the law was breathing down their necks, he had burned the trunk containing the venison and was convicted of arson. I don't remember all the details after all these years, but it was a funny coincidence at the time.

Lyle had a great sense of humor, and when something struck him in an amusing manner, he would laugh for days every time he thought of it. One incident that amused him no end, though it could have had a tragic ending, turned out, fortunately, without tragedy.

An old man had gone out deer hunting alone down in the Machias area. When it became dark and he hadn't returned home, the wardens were notified and went out to search for him. The search went on for two days with no sign of his whereabouts. Luckily, the weather stayed quite warm for November. Finally, on the third day, the wardens came upon him sitting on a stump in the middle of a small clearing, with his boots and socks off, cutting his toenails with a hunting knife. His feet were all squizzled and wrinkled as his boots had been constantly full of water from wading across streams. His toenails were so long they curled about a half-inch under his toes. There he sat trying to pare them down with that long hunting knife. Lyle said they curled down just like bird talons and were as hard and tough as leather. Every time he thought of that poor old codger sitting on that

that stump whittling away on his toenails, he went into a gale of laughter. The old fellow didn't even look up when the wardens came upon him. He was oblivious to the fact that they had been searching for him for over two days. All he could think of was getting his toenails trimmed. Fortunately, he was none the worse for wear, even after having spent two cold nights in the woods.

Oftentimes Lyle himself was the central character in many an amusing incident, some of which I will relate.

When Robert Fulton invented the steamboat, it was dubbed "Fulton's Folly." So it was when Lyle decided to buy a forty-three-foot cabin cruiser to use on Long Pond. Now, Long Pond is by no means an expansive body of water, even though it is one of the largest lakes on the island. It is approximately five miles long and a mile wide at its widest point. There are many shallow and rocky areas and one can get into enough trouble in a rowboat, let alone a boat of that size. Thus it came about that the cruiser *Laura* was referred to as "Lyle's Folly," most specifically by my mother, Zettie. As I've said before, Lyle was given to champagne tastes on a beer income and generally acquired whatever he set out to obtain, usually much to the disapproval of my mother. He was always quick to spy a unique opportunity and decided the time was right to run sightseeing tours on the lake starting from Pond's End. The *Laura* was just the boat he was looking for. He bought her for about $250 at a local estate sale. She was a beautiful craft—needle-nosed, narrow of beam, and drew little water. She slipped through the water as lightly as a feather. Lyle built a long T-dock for her which would easily have accommodated the *Queen Mary*. This worked out to his advantage, though, as frequently, in docking, he needed plenty of maneuvering space to bring the *Laura* into her berth—no problem for a more experienced skipper.

The tours attracted many people and introduced them to a part of Acadia National Park which could only be seen from the water. By reservation, cocktail parties could be held aboard, with dinner being served later at Pond's End after the cruise. Many a passenger, occasionally including the captain, have I seen staggering up the dock after disembarking from the *Laura,* barely missing a dunk in the lake. However, I don't recall anyone ever going overboard, though that was just pure luck.

Lyle was always the most gracious host dressed in his spotless white captain's uniform. He was a striking character—tall, handsome, with piercing blue eyes—a colorful personality, who regaled his passengers with his interesting and concise dissertations on nature and the descriptions of various points of interest around the lake.

One day as the *Laura* had reached the main part of the lake where the mountains on either side seem to rise directly from the water, he was relating to his passengers how once or twice he had seen a bald eagle swoop off the mountaintop and grasp a sea gull in flight right out of the air. Just as he spoke the words, a huge eagle soared from the mountaintop and attacked a sea gull on the wing. There pursued a life and death struggle for a few seconds, then the eagle, being the victor, flew off to its aerie with the gull dangling limply from his sharp talons. The passengers gasped in disbelief.

Everyone loved Lyle's "pomp and circumstance." He was a born actor and inherently knew how and when to turn on the charm.

The day the *Laura* was launched was a never-to-be-forgotten one. It was just before the Fourth of July and Lyle wanted to launch her before the holiday. There she sat in her cradle on the shore at Pond's End awaiting her baptism: forty-three feet of sparkling white paint above a bright blue bottom. On her stern, Old Glory waved and fluttered in anticipation, adding grandeur to the name painted in large black and gold letters below.

A big crowd had gathered to see the only cabin cruiser ever to be launched on Long Pond. Norman Bouchard, a boat builder from Southwest Harbor, was

The Laura *with Cap'n Smith aboard (above) and at the helm.*

the man in charge of this operation. Lyle was aboard on the afterdeck holding forth in grand style, his captain's hat set at a jaunty angle. As soon as Norm had the rollers under her hull, Lyle commanded, "She's ready, Norm. Let 'er roll!" Norm obeyed and the craft rolled the few feet into the water. Then came a grinding, screeching crash with Lyle dangling over the stern, hanging on for dear life with one arm. The ship nearly rolled on her side as the cradle broke under her.

"Jump, Lyle! Jump!" yelled Norm.

"Jump, hell and be damned!" shouted Lyle as he scrambled back aboard. "A good captain always stays with his ship."

Fate was surely on his side that day, for at that very moment the stern struck water just deep enough to right her and she floated free and upright. The crowd on the shore sent up a hearty cheer, horns tooted, and *Laura,* with Captain Smith at the helm, was off on her maiden voyage, escorted by a squadron of small boats flocking around her like a duck with her brood of ducklings. As surely as the night the *Titanic* sank was a night to remember, so was the day the *Laura* was launched, a day to remember. People who witnessed the event still talk about it today.

One night Lyle was taking a young man and his girl friend on a moonlight cruise aboard the *Laura.* He had sailed about a half-mile from the cove at Pond's End when he decided to go below and close the portholes, as the weather had turned a bit chilly. There wasn't a ripple on the water, so he felt confident in leaving the helm momentarily to go below. No sooner had he gotten down when there came a loud *scrunch.* All was quiet for a few seconds, then the young man yelled, "Cap'n Smith, I think we're aground!" Lyle poked his head up from the cabin like a chipmunk from his hole, with a look of disbelief on his face. "My God! How did that happen so fast?"

Well, there they sat. It was nearly midnight. No one was around to rescue them that late at night. Finally, a cottage owner who had not yet retired noticed the lights from the *Laura,* which seemed a bit off course—not in the channel where she should be. He watched for a minute and saw that she wasn't moving, so he phoned my mother at Pond's End. "Zettie," he exclaimed, "I think Lyle's aground down the lake on the west side. The *Laura* doesn't seem to be in the channel and she's standing still."

My mother then called my brother, Les, in Somesville, to come to the rescue. His wife sleepily answered the phone. "Mary, tell Les his father's aground. We need him to help."

Mary frantically shook Les from a sound sleep. "Leslie, wake up! Your mother just called and your father is *drowned!* She needs you at once!"

Les drove the two miles in record time, racing into the parking lot at Pond's End in a swirl of dust and gravel, prepared for the worst. There was Mom, cool as a cucumber, washing the dishes while she waited. Les, white as a ghost and shaking like a leaf, yelled, "Dad's drowned! My God, what happened?"

Mom, in her usual unruffled manner, said, "Drowned? I told Mary he was aground, not drowned." With a huge sigh of relief which left him as limp as a rag, Les proceeded to rescue the passengers, who were completely unperturbed by their experience. They had a great time and loved all the excitement. Lyle stayed aboard all night after seeing his passengers safely into the rescue boat. As he said before, "A good captain always stays with his ship."

The next morning, the *Laura,* luckily unscathed, was put back afloat. All the damage that was done was to Lyle's ego. After that episode, the *Laura* was nicknamed "African Queen," as the young man who had anticipated a moonlight cruise had been involved in the production of the movie, *The African Queen,* which at that time was very popular.

Lyle used the *Laura* for a couple of summers and then he found a twenty-eight-foot lobster boat, which he thought would be better adapted to his sightseeing tours, and much more maneuverable and practical for use on the lake. She was called *Aloha.*

One early evening, a group of friends were aboard the *Aloha,* including my husband, our children and me. We had reached the southern end of the lake where we planned to drop anchor and have a picnic aboard. At that end of the lake, there's a certain area that is very rocky, where large boulders lurk about a foot below the surface. Lyle was explaining to my husband that one had to be very careful navigating here because of the big rocks. Suddenly, my husband let out a yell, "Watch out, Lyle! You're getting in too close!" At that moment came a terrible *klunk* and we thought the bottom had been torn asunder.

"For God's sake, Lyle, back 'er down! You're on the rocks!" screamed my husband.

Lyle, undaunted, and who had been doing more talking than watching just where he was going, snapped back, "I know it! I'm just showing you where they are!" He could never be outdone. It was against his nature.

It was another close call, but again the boat emerged undamaged.

That same evening, as we were returning from our cruise, a gorgeous full moon rose over the lake, bathing the world about us in a silvery sheen. The water was like a mirror, not a breath of air stirred and there was complete silence on board. Everyone was absorbed in the breathtaking beauty of the night. As we approached the channel, Lyle somehow became confused and got on the wrong side of the channel marker and we hit shoal water. Another grinding, scraping halt! "Dammit," exploded Lyle, "if those kids back there would stop their damn noise and the nor'west wind wouldn't blow me off course, I *might* get this ship back to the dock!" The kids had been asleep for two hours and the lake was like glass. We were all silently shaking with laughter, not daring to make a peep and offend our host. Captain

Smith was having enough trouble getting back on the right side of the channel marker and it would have been quite a swim to Pond's End. Both the *Laura* and the *Aloha* had more lives than a cat.

My husband, having spent four years at sea in World War II, was quite experienced in navigation. Whenever he suggested something to Lyle that would help him navigate, Lyle would snappily retort, "Who'n hell's captain of this ship, anyway, St. Louis? You or me?" My husband (with tongue in cheek) chided him, to get his reaction, which was usually explosive. He had a short fuse in that respect. However, they were the closest of friends and their bickering amused the passengers no end. They adored it!

12

One day in early June Lyle was painting boats and working around Pond's End preparing for the summer season, when a young couple stopped to ask directions to a camp they had rented on the lake. They were New Yorkers and obviously not at all acquainted with the "wilds of Maine." Lyle graciously gave them the directions they requested. They lingered on, asking questions about the island and interspersing remarks such as, "It's sure in the boonies around here. Doesn't seem to be much to see or do that's very interesting. We had no idea it was this dead or we'd have gone some other place where there's excitement and something to see."

As they continued to talk, Lyle grew hotter and hotter under the collar. Damned city slickers! They didn't even recognize the natural beauty of this spot—this beloved island. He sure didn't need that kind of tourist around here. If they wanted excitement why didn't they go to Coney Island?

The next morning, bright and early, Lyle was again painting his boats when the same young couple drove up looking wild-eyed and in a noticeable dither, their car squealing to a halt when they spied Lyle. "Mr. Smith," they asked excitedly, "can you tell us what kind of an animal would make those awful screeching and screaming and wailing sounds we heard all night long? We didn't sleep a wink!"

Lyle, knowing full well that it was loons calling one another, replied, "Oh, sure. That's a timber wolf. There's a small pack of them on that side of the lake."

The young couple's eyes bugged out and their mouths fell open. At that instant, the young man happened to look up to see my mother draping a couple of white fur rugs over the railing of the upstairs deck for airing.

"Wh-wh-what kind of animal skins are those?" he asked.

"Oh, those are polar bear skins," informed Lyle.

"You have polar bears around here, too?" he asked, not quite believing his ears.

"Sure do. Why some winters when it gets too cold in the Arctic they'll travel this far south to find warmer temperatures. Those skins are from two I killed on the lake here, a few years back."

The young man turned to his wife, a look of horror on his face, grabbed her by the arm and shouted, "Let's get the hell out of this God-forsaken place! It's too wild for me! Polar bears! Wolves!"

Off they sped, dust and gravel flying out behind them. Lyle returned to his painting, chuckling with laughter and self-satisfaction. He'd sure cooked their goose. Ah, revenge, how sweet!

Later, on this very same day, Lyle had another experience which he didn't soon forget. In fact, it was his main topic of conversation for the next six months.

Just before noon, a big black Cadillac convertible pulled up, driven by a very beautiful young woman: "a beautiful piece of humanity" as Lyle would say. She was accompanied by two pre-teenage children, and was obviously looking for a place to swim. She asked Lyle if they could swim there and he promptly told her they could swim to their hearts' content. Then he did a double take, looked at the lady intently for a moment, and said, "You look very familiar. I've seen you somewhere before."

She flashed a bright smile, then replied, "Maybe on TV. I'm on the "I've Got a Secret" show."

"That's it!" he retorted with quite some excitement as he extended his hand. "My name's Lyle Smith. TV doesn't do you justice, though. I always watch your show." He was all a-flutter having met such a prominent star.

"Is there a place where I can change into my bathing suit?" she inquired.

"Well, there's a little thicket across the road that's pretty secluded. You'll see a little path right over there," he said, pointing.

She presently returned and with the two children spent most of the afternoon swimming and sunning. She was quite something in her shiny black bathing suit and Lyle's eyes strayed in her direction quite frequently. I'm sure there was more paint on the ground than on the boat he was painting that day.

When it came time to leave, she went again to the thicket across the road to change. In those few minutes a tar truck came by spreading thick, gooey tar all along the road. As she emerged from the path and spied that spread of black goo, she let out a shriek that could be heard for a mile. "Mr. Smith, help, help! How do I get across the road? I'm barefoot, too. Oh, dear!"

Now Lyle was never one to refuse help to a damsel, especially one in distress. So he slogged across the road, swept the beautiful lady up in his arms and carried her happily to the other side where she thanked him profusely. He allowed that the pleasure had all been his despite the load of tar on his boots, new ones at that.

In all the excitement of her dilemma with the tar, she had dropped her towel. Lyle later found it and hung it in the bathroom. He used it all summer and cautioned my mother not to dare put it into the laundry as long as there was even a trace of the lady's perfume lingering on it. My mother amusedly humored him since it was only the lady's towel she had to worry about.

The "beautiful lady," by the way, was the glamorous TV personality, Jayne Meadows.

On another evening in early July, Lyle and Zettie had just managed some time to sit down to a late dinner after a busy day in the restaurant when the phone started frantically ringing. As Lyle answered, a tearful, distraught female voice whimpered, "Mr. Smith, have you seen my monkey?"

Lyle hesitated for a second, then blurted out, "Have I seen your wh-a-at?"

The girl went on to explain, sobbing all the while, that she had arrived that day to spend two weeks at a nearby cottage and had brought her pet monkey along. Somehow the monkey had managed to open his cage door and had escaped into the woods. The last she saw of him, he was headed in the direction of Pond's End.

Lyle, his blue eyes twinkling at the thought of a monkey loose in the woods, informed her that he had seen no such creature, but would keep a watchful eye out for him. As he hung up the phone, he was laughing uncontrollably. "I'll be doggoned! A monkey loose in the woods around here! That's a good one!"

The next morning when Lyle went outside, there sat Mr. Monkey on a limb overhanging the water, chattering and scolding away. No amount of coaxing with bananas could budge him. Finally he left, still chattering, swinging jungle fashion, from treetop to treetop.

All that summer he was frequently spotted by hikers and sightseers, but somehow he always managed to elude any would-be captors. Needless to say, people were indeed surprised to see a monkey flitting about in the forests of Mount Desert.

Soon the golden glint of late August arrived with its chilly nights which certainly didn't enhance the comfort of a jungle creature. Then one autumnlike morning, a chicken farmer, who lived about five miles from Pond's End, called Lyle to say that he had caught the little runaway. It seems that when the farmer went to the henhouse to gather eggs, he felt something furry in a nest. Huddled beneath a hen, keeping warm, was the monkey! No wonder the hens had been acting strange lately and cackling at unusual times.

Lyle then notified the monkey's mistress, who lived in New York. She was ecstatic and agreed to be there on the upcoming weekend to collect him.

In the meantime, Lyle kept the monkey in his cage in the *Aloha*'s cabin right next to the engine. If the weather had a bit of a chill, he started up the engine to keep the monkey warm. His owner arrived at the stated time and took her little charge home to the big city. That must have been a decided change for him. What a summer of freedom he had enjoyed until the chill of autumn tinged the air!

Then there was the time that Zettie sent Lyle to the fish pier in Southwest Harbor to pick up the lobsters she needed to serve at lunch time. As he was walking down the gangplank to the pier, a scraggly-looking individual approached him from the opposite direction. This person was dressed in faded bluejeans and a tentlike red and black checkered shirt, with the shirttail outside over the preponderance of his midsection. He sported a long bushy black beard, the hippie type, seldom seen at that time—the middle fifties. Lyle, in direct contrast, was dressed in his crisp suntan captain's uniform, all spit and polish, as usual.

As this unkempt rotund character drew near, he stopped, waggled his forefinger right under Lyle's nose and shouted very emphatically, "Twentieth Century Fox wants you!"

Hesitantly, Lyle looked him over for a minute, then blurted out, "Who in hell is Twentieth Century Fox?" He was never a movie buff as you can see.

The man explained, "It's a very well-known movie production company in Hollywood—in fact, world-known. I'd like to see you here this afternoon at two for a screen test. You're just the character we're looking for!"

Lyle, completely flabbergasted, and not believing his ears, exclaimed, "I'll be here!"

Fifteen minutes later his car squealed to a stop at Pond's End. With long, resolute strides to the back door, he threw it open and solemnly announced, "I'm going to be in the movies!" He then proceeded to relate to us in his melodramatic manner his encounter with the movie scout, all the while his blue eyes snapping sparks of excitement.

Zettie, who had witnessed many a similar episode, calmly continued lunch preparations, seemingly oblivious to Lyle's dissertation. "Lyle, where are my lobsters?" she inquired. "It's nearly time for the noon rush."

At that point, Lyle looked a bit sheepish. "Oh, my God! I forgot 'em after meeting that movie scout!"

Well, I don't need to tell you that Lyle was at the pier in Southwest Harbor way before the appointed hour of two. He waited, and he waited, and he waited. When 4:00 P.M. finally rolled around, he decided that his movie career had ended before it had even begun since no movie scout had shown up. No one in the vicinity had even seen a character filling his description that afternoon, either. Another pipe dream gone to glory!

13

One evening some friends were having dinner at Pond's End, after which my husband, Tom, and I joined them for coffee. Later, Lyle joined us with the news that a well-known resident of the town had just passed away.

After some discussion about the attributes of the deceased, Tom spoke up, saying, "Lyle, it's about time you and Zettie started to think about getting a cemetery plot while you're both still around to let us know about it." This was not a new subject to be broached to Lyle and it annoyed him no end. Tom had been raised with the idea that one should always make sure, before his demise, that he had a place to rest his bones. Therefore he often badgered Lyle about being prepared for the day he departed.

Now Lyle never liked to be reminded that this day would eventually arrive for him, as well as any other mortal being. He absolutely refused to make a will, regardless of how much advice he was given. Even on his deathbed when he knew he was dying, he could not bring himself to do it. This, of course, did not make things easier for Zettie.

When Tom mentioned the word "cemetery," Lyle flew into a rage, waving his arms about and yelling, "Don't mention cemeteries to me," his temper still flaring. "I'm going to be cremated and my ashes buried under God's green trees. No cemetery is goin' to fence me in!"

Tom always received the same reaction from him and enjoyed riling him up to see how volatile he would become.

About six years later, Lyle became terminally ill with cancer. The nine months before his death were difficult ones for our family. Each of us tried to put his best foot forward and to go about the routine of life as normally as possible. We never discussed death with him or even inferred for one moment that we doubted his recovery. He avoided the subject, too. Outwardly, he showed no sign of depression and was always his jovial self. It seemed to me that he thought if no one acknowledged the fact that he was terminally ill, the cancer would go away. He went about his daily activities normally, seeming to fight for life with bulldog determination. He had undergone surgery in early spring for the removal of a lung, and did make a remarkable recovery. However, by early autumn, he seemed to be regressing.

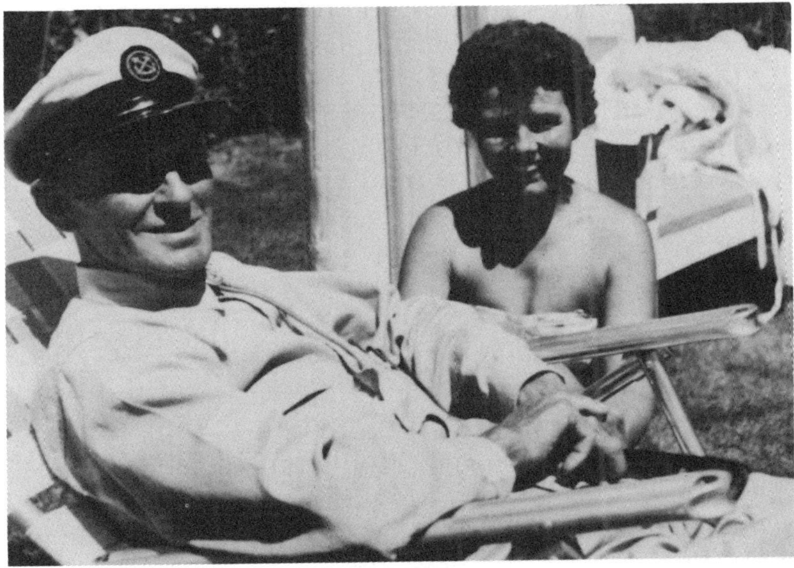

Lyle and Lyla at Pond's End three months before his death in December, 1961.

We often found him sitting by the lake in his car, gazing at the view before him, lost in deep thought. Later that fall, after Pond's End had closed for the season, he would drive there and sit for hours as if unable to absorb enough of the beauty around him and the spot he dearly loved. Sometimes, near the end, he became so exhausted from just the short drive from home to lake, he didn't have the strength for the return trip. Then Zettie would become alarmed and would go searching for him. He was always found there—just sitting and looking at the lake.

By Thanksgiving of 1961 he had grown steadily weaker and had to take to his bed. He fought this with a vengeance but there was no avoiding it now: he was physically unable to keep going. By then the doctor had told us that he couldn't go on more than a few weeks. On December 18, 1961, he passed away after a fight to the finish. Never once did he give up the battle.

Sometime during those lingering months he had mentioned to Zettie that if he went before she did (he still would not accept the seriousness of his illness), he wanted to be cremated and have his dear friend, Brownie, the coastal warden pilot, scatter his ashes over Long Pond. This was contrary to his earlier statements about being buried under God's green trees. Possibly his love of flying entered into it.

The weather, the week of his death, was very stormy and miserable. It rained and snowed, then froze solidly. Driving was practically at a standstill and as treacherous as could be. That didn't stop people from calling, however. Many came from miles away. I remember one fellow who came to the door the night before the funeral. He had driven all the way from Millinocket and how he ever made it is a mystery to me. The driving was so hazardous, and to top that, he had been imbibing quite heavily. My mother answered the door and he grabbed her in a big bear hug, sobbing uncontrollably. "Lyle Smith was one of the finest officers I've ever known and I'll always call him my best friend." Great sobs racked him and Zettie invited him in to have something to eat and a cup of coffee. He sat for a while and sobered up considerably. In all the confusion, we didn't ask his name nor did he volunteer it. To this day, we don't know what Lyle ever did for him or why he traveled such a great distance under such hazardous conditions. At the services the next day, there he sat as near the front as possible, big tears streaming down his cheeks.

If God ever created a setting to befit a passing soul, he certainly outdid himself the day of Lyle's funeral. The night before, it had rained, then turned colder and froze. Before morning, heavy wet snow fell and clung to the ice, weighting down trees and limbs. We awoke to a winter wonderland. The trees, bent under their snow burden, stretched heavy limbs against the clear blue sky. The whole world sparkled with myriads of diamonds as the morning sun rose to greet the day. On the way to the service, the stately elms bordering each side of the street in the little village of Somesville were so heavily laden with snow and ice, that their branches drooped over the street, creating an alabaster cavern studded with billions of sparkling jewels. I have never to this day seen such glorious and spectacular winter scenes. I felt that the good Lord had planned it that way, knowing Lyle's deep love of nature and his commitment to its preservation—a sendoff of rare magnificence.

As we drove home after the service, the snow began to melt and fall from the trees. It had held up just long enough to provide a background of splendor for a departing soul who so truly appreciated God's handiwork.

Because the weather continued to be harsh that winter, we decided to wait until spring to dispose of Lyle's ashes. As warm weather approached, my mother said to me one day, "You know, I've been thinking about your father's ashes. I don't think we should ask Brownie to scatter them over the lake. In the first place, it would be a very emotional thing for him. You know how much he thought of your father. In the second place, every time I'd see a speck floating in the lake, I'd think, 'That could be Lyle'."

She suggested we put them in a special spot where our family had camped and picnicked when we were children—a place we all loved and had great sentiment for. Then she informed us that she, too, wanted to be cremated and her ashes mingled with his when the time came. We all agreed that was the sensible thing to do as we could visit the spot whenever we wished.

The day we chose for the burial was a gorgeous June day—Lyle's birthday, in fact. We rounded up as many of his progeny as were available—children and grandchildren. It was quite a long hike through the woods to reach the chosen spot. Everyone took a turn carrying the small box that contained "Gramp's ashes," except his four-year-old grandson, Bobby, whose short legs were struggling to keep up with our so-called cortege. After some minutes, when we were nearing our destination, Bobby stopped dead in his tracks and yelled in an exasperated tone, "Gee whiz, you guys! I wish you'd let me carry Gramp for a while."

Lyle would have been happy could he have known who his pallbearers were and the unceremonious way in which he was borne to his final resting place. This is what he loved—no ceremony and surrounded by those he loved.

So now he lies "under God's green trees" with no fences hemming him in. My mother and brother, Bob, have now joined him and they rest in the quiet solitude of the place they all loved.

Thus ends the saga of an old-time game warden—a life of experiences and adventures that most men who love the out-of-doors would envy.

EPILOGUE

In this summer of 1990, twenty-five years after Pond's End's door was closed for the last time, I sit on my dock across the cove, watching the activity there. It is pleasing to know that my parents, Lyle and Zettie Smith, made this spot available to the public. Now a small unobtrusive sign designates it as The Town of Mount Desert Recreational Area. Few of its visitors know the history and the wonderful times that happened there.

Scenes and echoes of the past flash before me. I see Lyle in his warden days snowshoeing up the lake on a cold winter's day, his red "Mounties" coat a bright splash of color against the snowy landscape. I see him taking off and landing his little Aeronica Chief on the ice after qualifying for his pilot's license when he was over fifty. As he alights from the cockpit, his blue eyes sparkle and he flashes a happy, satisfied grin, knowing he has accomplished a dream of many years—to own and fly a plane.

The sound of the outboard on his Old Town canoe penetrates my consciousness, as he comes bobbing up the lake in the throes of a southeast gale of nearly hurricane force that has caused my mother a few hours of anxiety, though Lyle, himself, is completely unconcerned about any imminent danger.

As I watch the happy groups of people canoeing, sailing, windsurfing, swimming, or just enjoying the peace and tranquility of their surroundings, Lyle's words dart through my mind: "I hope the public will have access to this place forever, so everyone can enjoy its beauty."

In my mind's eye I see the *Laura* or the *Aloha* pulling away from the dock, filled with happy sightseers, gliding smoothly down the lake, Lyle's voice trailing out behind. "Ladies and gentlemen, you are about to behold one of the most beautiful and unspoiled areas of Mount Desert Island. Directly ahead you will observe. . . . "

My thoughts drift off into oblivion with memories of an unforgettable era—times, lives, and places remembered.

L.E.S.L.
Long Pond, MDI
July 1990